BEHIND THE
PLEXIGLASS

*THROUGH THE LENS
OF A* **FAST FOOD WORKER**
DURING THE PANDEMIC

RAINNA ANCHETA

Behind the Plexiglass

Copyright © 2025 by Rainna Ancheta.

All rights reserved. No part of this publication may be reproduced, distributed, or transmitted in any form or by any means, including photocopying, recording, or other electronic or mechanical methods, without the written consent of the publisher. The only exceptions are for brief quotations included in critical reviews and other noncommercial uses permitted by copyright law.

MILTON & HUGO L.L.C.
4407 Park Ave., Suite 5
Union City, NJ 07087, USA

Website: *www.miltonandhugo.com*
Hotline: *1- 888-778-0033*
Email: *info@miltonandhugo.com*

Ordering Information:
Quantity sales. Special discounts are granted to corporations, associations, and other organizations. For more information on these discounts, please reach out to the publisher using the contact information provided above.

Library of Congress Control Number:	2025900066	
ISBN-13:	979-8-89285-212-8	[Paperback Edition]
	979-8-89285-213-5	[Hardback Edition]
	979-8-89285-214-2	[Digital Edition]

Rev. date: 01/31/2025

TO MY FAMILY
DAD, MOM, AND BIG BROTHERS
Thank you for supporting me.

CONTENTS

Author's Note xi
Prologue xiii

PART 1 PRE - PANDEMIC TO FIRST WAVE OF THE PANDEMIC 1
1 The Interview 3
2 The Work Process 9
3 Bruno 11
4 Life Unexpectedly 21
5 13th March 2020 24
6 Adapting to New Safety Protocols 29
7 The Pause 35
8 Customer's excuses 41
9 The Virus Was Scared of Him 45
10 Out Of Ketchup 47
11 Sunny Day 55
12 Uncontrolled Behaviour 65
13 A Frustrated Nurse 68
14 Fish Market 71
15 Appreciative Customer 74
16 Slow Day 78
17 Rainy Sunday 82
18 Deliveries Were Not Available 88
19 Heart Broken 91

PART 2 THE PEOPLE INSIDE THE FAST FOOD 95
20 The Good Supervisors 97
21 Lolita 104
22 Religious Martin 111
23 Mariano 115
24 PCR and Isolated 121
25 Back To Work 134

PART 3 SECOND WAVE BEGUN TO BUILD UP 139
26 Online College School 141
27 Entitled Customers... 145
28 Black Socks Only 148
29 My Work Hat... 151
30 Bad Days 155
31 Cystic Acne 165
32 Mental Health 169
33 Therapy 172
34 Blood Work.. 176
35 Uber Rides.. 179

PART 4 THE SECOND WAVE PEAKED IN
MID-JANUARY 2021, THEN EASED. 187
36 My Heart Ripped..189
37 "I'm not coming back here anymore"........................192
38 Hospital Visit...196
39 Antonio Disliked Me 198
40 The Increased Prices...203
41 The Good Customers...207
42 College Placement..211
43 Failed Exam 215

PART 5 NTH TIME WAVE 2022 221
44 Heavy Snow 223
45 "Remind your staff to smile."....................................230
46 Downtime 238
47 Be Patient 242
48 Life Outside Of Work 248
49 Betrayal 251
50 Forgiving 258
51 Goodbye, Bruno 260
52 Carpe Diem 264
53 Our True Work Is Looking After One Another.......268
54 Goodbye, Fast-Food 273
55 Pandemic Reflection...278

Conclusion..283
Acknowledgement..285
Praise For Behind The Plexiglass 287
About The Author..291
Social Media..293

Author's Note

Behind the Plexiglass is my debut memoir. I poured my soul and heart into it. I saved my journal during the pandemic and Instagram and Facebook Stories to look back on. I contacted some of my co-workers during that period and asked them what they remembered to help me remember what had happened and see if I remembered them correctly. They were helpful, but they all had a side note saying, "I don't wanna remember the awful years of the pandemic."

Some names mentioned in this story are pseudonyms, and some have permitted me to put their name.

Prologue

I got a new job at a fast-food restaurant before the COVID-19 outbreak, but before the world shut down, I lived an everyday life where I went to work, hung out with friends, and worked on myself.

Coronavirus or COVID-19 is the disease caused by the SARS-CoV-2 coronavirus. It usually spreads quickly between people in close contact. Symptoms don't show up until fourteen days after contracting the virus.

The first case was found in Wuhan, China, in November 2019. It was said to have come from a bat. Most people infected with the virus will experience mild to moderate respiratory illness and recover without requiring special treatment. However, some will become seriously ill and require medical attention, especially those who are old age, people with asthma, diabetes, and other serious illnesses that, when they catch COVID-19, can be deadly.

I was on my way to my kickboxing classes when I got a notification from my dad on Facebook asking how I was doing. I didn't feel like replying to him; I thought I would answer when I got on the bus. While waiting for the bus to come, I scrolled through my social media and saw a lot of posts about the coronavirus spreading in China.

'Na-ah, that ain't reaching Canada.' I thought.

At the age of twenty-one, I realized I needed to embrace new challenges and focus on self-improvement. I realized I needed to start figuring things out as I entered adulthood. This epiphany prompted me to embark on a fitness journey, work a little harder, start a skincare routine and expand my horizons. In addition to continuing my gym routine,

I wanted to broaden my horizons by enrolling in kickboxing and rock climbing classes to maintain an active lifestyle.

By December 2019, I had set clear goals for the upcoming year (2020). I aimed to sustain my physical activity, adopt a healthier diet, have a good skincare routine to maintain good skin and diligently work towards paying off my debts.

However, pondering about my aspirations in life, I realized that my current income needs to increase. Working just 15 hours a week at an office job was insufficient to sustain my personal needs, and I struggled to make ends meet.

A train of thoughts ran through my mind as I sat on the bus, and my only therapy was writing down my emotions and going to kickboxing classes.

When I got the job at a fast-food company as my second job, I was grateful, and I couldn't help but feel an overwhelming sense of gratitude for the opportunity. I thought I would be able to pay off my debts since I would be working two jobs, and I would be able to reach my fitness goals and good skincare routine goals, but little did I know that every goal I wrote down by December of 2019 would be wiped out when the pandemic hit.

The WHO (World Health Organization) declared the global pandemic on March 11, 2020, and announced that some essential workers, such as construction workers, hospital staff, fast-food workers, grocery store workers and others, would stay to work. Some were forced to stay at home, some lost their job and received Employment Insurance benefits. The Employment Insurance (E.I.) program provides temporary income support to unemployed workers seeking employment. I wanted to stay home and rely on E.I. benefits, but I needed to socialize, so I chose to work. They closed down small businesses, gyms, malls, and other establishments.

Some restaurants and bookstores were temporarily closed during the pandemic, and some were permanently closed. Some of my friends who go to the gym complained about closing the gym since it should be considered essential. Eight customers in our fast-food restaurant were considered "too crowded."

We all had to wait for someone to leave the store before we let someone come in to order food. Some customers would scream at us for not letting them in, even when we had explained our protocol. We were all scared to go outside because we might catch the virus, and we didn't want to bring the coronavirus to our family.

We have moved from seeing one another at coffee shops to phone calls and video chatting. We used to talk in person but shared Instagram reels or TikTok videos to stay connected. We stopped watching T.V. in the summer of 2020 because the news about the virus spread was too much to take, and we tried to loosen up a bit and enjoy our summer.

Overall, 2020 was rough, and it has changed a lot. It was not easy, but we made it. Not everyone was lucky enough to make it alive because they caught the deadly virus, hence resulting in the death of so many people, which breaks my heart.

PART I

PRE - PANDEMIC TO FIRST WAVE OF THE PANDEMIC

1
THE INTERVIEW

"Rainna, you have an interview with the manager Antonio on the 7th at one o'clock, that's on Tuesday. Don't forget." Scott said this in a voice message on Instagram during the first week of January 2020.

My forehead felt intense, and I replayed Scott's voice message a few times more. I took a moment to think if Scott was serious about it. Then I replied to chat messages,

"For real? Why didn't they call me?"

Then, Scott replied, "Well, my brother is close to the manager. So, they told my brother that you have an interview."

"What is your brother's name? He works there?" I asked Scott.

"His name is Ralph," he replied.

"Oh, okay. Thank you, Scott! I greatly appreciate it," I replied to Scott.

I took a deep breath. I was confused and had so many questions in mind. I took time to figure out how the fast-food restaurant that I applied for didn't call me to let me know that I had an interview with them; instead, they verbally told Scott's brother that they'd schedule me for an interview. Because of that, I had a bad impression of their fast-food restaurant.

Nonetheless, I grinned and screamed, "Yes!" I jumped up and down in my room alone, excitedly and feeling giddy about the thought that I'd be having a job interview soon. I could feel my heartbeat rapidly. I imagined greeting the customers and socializing with other people.

Days had gone by, and it was already Tuesday. I was reading the news about the coronavirus on my phone as I walked to the bus stop on my way to the fast-food interview. I closed my phone off and crossed the road. The road was busy, and a car was honking at the car in front of it, which stopped to make the right turn while I was crossing the road. I was shocked when cars blew their horns.

It was a half-hour bus ride, and I missed my stop. I had to walk from the bus stop to the fast-food location for ten minutes. When I got there, I lined up with two other customers. There were two cashiers in front. I wondered who I should approach regarding my job interview.

When it was my turn, the cashier, who looked like a young adult, perhaps my age at 21, waved at me and said, "Good afternoon, welcome to Fast Food; how may I help you?" She looked at the screen monitor in front of her, ready to place an order for me.

"Hi! I have an interview with Antonio at one o'clock," I told the cashier. The cashier looked at the clock, which said 12:50 in the afternoon and went to the office room. Two workers were preparing food orders, and a supervisor bagged the order. When she returned to the front, the storefront supervisor named Nelia asked the cashier, "What happened?"

"She said she has an interview with Antonio, but I can't find him." the cashier said, pointing at me. The supervisor turned to me and said, "Just have a seat there, and he will come to you." She pointed her index finger at the chairs in front of the counter.

"Okay, thank you!" I said, and then I sat and waited.

I sat on the chair and felt uneasy; I had mixed feelings of excitement and fear. The counter staff were busy, and they had a vast line-up. One of the customer's kids was holding a pink balloon and asked his parents for ice cream; her parents were busy on their phones. Sitting on the chair and staring into nothingness, I thought, 'I wished I could go back in time holding a pink balloon just like that kid and ask Mom for an ice cream, but here I am, waiting for a job interview.'

The store had music playing somewhere, but I could not hear the song since it was noisy in the fast food, and most of the customers were laughing. Some were taking pictures, and I thought, 'Will I be able to work here?'. It looked busier than the previous fast-food restaurant where I used to work. Regardless, I had a gut feeling that I would get the job, but I couldn't believe that the fast-food manager was unprofessional for not telling me directly that I had an interview.

Sitting there for half an hour, I itched to check my phone, scroll through social media, and see what was happening in Australia since one of my online friends lives there. I saw a couple of notifications from Facebook and five messages on Instagram. I didn't want to check my messages on social media since I didn't want any distractions. I watched people come and leave the restaurant. I watched the workers cleaning the tables with spray bottles and microfibre rugs. I was trying to avoid making eye contact with the front supervisor, Nelia, who was ten feet away from me, because I didn't want them to think that I was getting bored. But I stayed for almost an hour since I was eager to get this job and needed it to sustain my personal needs.

Forty-eight minutes later, I was sitting in the same chair, waiting for the manager to come out of the office and interview me. I did not know his voice, nor had I seen his appearance.'

'Should I leave?' I thought, 'But I need this job.'

The family with a kid holding the pink balloon arrived at the fast-food restaurant after I arrived. I saw them leaving after dining in, yet here I am, still seated on my chair, waiting to be called for my interview with Antonio.

As I read the menu board for the hundredth time, I accidentally locked eyes with Nelia. She went to the office. Then, she approached me and said, "He'll be here soon. Sorry about your wait."

I nodded and said, "That's okay. Thank you."

I was hungry, and I only had coffee that day. *'They better hire me,'* I thought.

Ten minutes later, a man with a nice haircut, about 5'6 ft tall and skinny, approached me. After over 50 minutes of sitting, I stood up and felt dizzy. *'Do I need to shake his hand as a greeting?'* I asked myself.

"Uhm, you can sit here on this side. Do you have a resume with you?" he asked.

I was puzzled and said, "No, I don't. I thought Ralph sent it to you through email.".

"Okay, just wait here." He said, and he looked disappointed.

I sat on the other side of the fast-food restaurant, near the exit door, and thought,

'Will this be another 50 minutes of waiting?'

He came after 10 minutes with my printed resume.

"Hello, is this "ray-na"?" Asking how to pronounce my name, I said, "It's 'rey-na'"

Then he looked through my resume and said, "So you worked from another fast food restaurant as a team leader?"

"Yes, I did. For five years." I answered.

"Why do you want to work here?" He asked with a strong Filipino accent while looking through my resume.

"I want to work here to contribute my skills since I have five years of experience in a different fast-food restaurant." I lied about wanting to contribute my skills. I just needed an extra income to pay off my credit cards.

He asked me two more questions but never made eye contact throughout the interview. "Are you a Filipino?"

"Yes, I am." I smiled at him.

"You speak Tagalog?"

"Yes, I do," I said.

Then he looked at me and said, "Do you have any questions?"

"Am I hired?" I asked and smiled.

He looked at me with a shock and a little smirk. He tried to hold his smile and said, "Well, the thing is, I want to hire you as a supervisor if you would like to. We promote people who are good enough to be supervisors, and as someone like you had previous experience, we would like to offer you a supervisory position. Would you be interested?"

I paused briefly. Memories from my previous fast-food job suddenly flashed in my thoughts. I had supervisory experience but knew I didn't want to be a supervisor at a fast-food restaurant since I was considering returning to college. Although it would be a good opportunity for me to become a supervisor, and it will look good on my resume, I don't want to take the supervisory position for granted if I accept it and then be busy being a student later on. I didn't want to use that position for my advantage because being a fast-food supervisor carries a huge responsibility and solid discipline, and I was not too fond of that maybe just yet.

"Uhm. No, I'm okay being a team member. Maybe in the future." I shrugged my shoulders and smiled. I declined his offer. I wanted to stay there only briefly since I had another job.

"Okay. No problem. Welcome to Fast Food." He said and smiled.

"Thank you. What's your name again? I'm sorry," I asked.

"Antonio."

I nodded. Then Antonio said, "We will contact you, and I will give you your schedule."

"Okay, thank you so much! Have a great day!"

I walked out of the store happy and went straight home. I messaged Scott, saying,

"Thank you so much, Scott, for sending my resume and telling me I had an interview. I got the job!!"

"Congratulations!! No problem!" Scott replied.

2

THE WORK PROCESS

Three days later, I got an email from the Fast Food company and read about the company policies and some videos to watch before I started my work shift. I wasn't sure if I should watch the videos since they didn't tell me anything.

'I think I need to watch 'em, since they sent it to me,' I thought.

Then, three weeks later, I was still waiting for Antonio to contact me.

One morning, before going to my office job, I searched for the store's number on Google and called Fast Food, but nobody answered. I tried calling them again around noon, and a lady who seemed to be one of the supervisors replied,

"Hello? Welcome to Fast Food! How may I help you?"

"Hello, it's Rainna, the new hire. Can I speak to Antonio, please?"

The lady on the other line said, "Antonio is not here today. He will be back on Monday. What is the reason for your call?"

"I just got the job three weeks ago and Antonio said he would contact me and give me a schedule, but I haven't heard anything from him since," I said nervously.

"Oh, okay. Call back on Monday. Thank you." Then, the lady on the other line hung up the phone. I looked through my house window blankly, I felt terrible.

As a new hire, I felt awful due to my new workplace's poor communication and management practices. I couldn't help but compare it to my previous job at a fast-food restaurant, where they communicated effectively and provided clear instructions for new hires. Regardless, I couldn't complain, but just had to swim with the uncertain waves of life.

When Monday came, I called Fast Food again and asked to speak with Antonio. A man's voice on the other line said, "Antonio, someone wanted to speak with you."

"Hello?" Antonio said.

"Hello, it's Rainna. You interviewed me on January 7th, and I'm still waiting for you to call me to confirm my schedule," I said.

"Uhmm. Okay. You can come tomorrow at five o'clock in the afternoon for training. What size is your uniform?" Antonio said.

"I think I'm size small." I answered.

"Okay, we have available uniform in that size. Come in tomorrow and ensure there are no long nails, okay?" Said he.

"Okay, Sounds good. Thank you so much!" I said. I hugged and kissed my cat excitedly. I was excited to finally work at a new fast-food restaurant. Although I wouldn't say I like to work late in the afternoon, I couldn't complain and just be grateful.

3

BRUNO

I went out with Bruno, whom I met on a dating app in December 2019, just before Christmas Eve. "What are you going to do tomorrow?" He asked on dating app messages.

"Nothing. Probably just clean the house." I said in a most boring response.

"Why are you cleaning the house? Leave that for the weekend," he said.

'He was right. Why would I clean on a Tuesday?' I thought.

He was handsome in the pictures but also looked like a bad boy since he wasn't smiling in his three photos on a dating app. It was my first time using a dating app. I was bored and wanted to see the hype about dating apps. I matched with about 15 people on the dating app, and I already went on a date with two men before Bruno. Some other guys would cancel, so it ended up having the last-minute bailout, resulting in a no-show.

When Bruno and I were chatting on the dating app, he asked for my Instagram account since it was easier to talk on social media than on a dating app's chat box. I could not even see the notifications from the dating app if someone messaged me, and perhaps Bruno had the same issue. I never wanted to date Bruno at first because I thought he was boring and immature. I couldn't imagine his appearance, but I wanted to meet him.

We started chatting about the holidays in December 2019, and he suddenly disappeared for a week. I thought we weren't going anywhere, but I didn't care much about Bruno since I also had other people to talk to.

I didn't pay much attention to the news about COVID-19, and I thought it wouldn't reach Canada. I posted a GoFundMe on Instagram since one of my friends in Southern Australia asked me to share a link to help people who had to move out due to wildfires that started in December 2019.

Then, Bruno returned to social media and messaged me;

"Hey, gorgeous. How have you been?" He came back the second week of January. Then, we started getting to know each other through Instagram. We both asked what we did for a living and what we liked to do in our free time.

"I am currently writing poems and would love to make them into a book one day, but I'm still figuring out the title." he said.

I barely knew writers in real life. Meeting Bruno, who loves writing made me feel more connected and comfortable with him.

One time, Bruno messaged me and asked, "Hey beautiful, how are you?" He always called me gorgeous, and it felt amazing to have someone call me gorgeous or beautiful.

I replied, "I'm stressed out with work and need to do some research for my office job. I just got a new job at a fast-food restaurant, so now I am working two jobs."

"It's 10:30 at night on a Thursday. Call it a day. It isn't worth it." Bruno replied.

That message made me feel at ease. I was stressed out while Bruno was calm.

'He's right; it's not worth it.' I thought. I closed my laptop, turned off my bedroom lights, and turned on the small humidifier in my room. I placed my phone on my study table and went to bed.

We exchanged messages the next day until, less than a month after talking on social media, he asked me for a date.

"When are you free?" said Bruno.

"I am free on Monday at around three o'clock in the afternoon after my kickboxing training. How about you?" I answered.

"I am free on Monday as well. Wanna go out?" he said.

"Yeah, for sure!"

"What do you want to do? Wanna go to the square or by the lake in Port Credit?" Bruno asked.

"I guess we can go by the lake and have coffee somewhere in the area."

"How about we go for dinner and walk by the lake?" Bruno suggested,

"Yeah, sounds good to me!"

"Okay, cool. I'll see you." he said. Then we stopped chatting on Instagram and only watched each other's Instagram stories.

When Monday came, I was in kickboxing training. I expected Bruno would cancel just like any other guy I met through a dating app before Bruno, who bailed out at the last minute. I didn't like Bruno much because he seemed solemn but had some humour, and I was also protecting myself from getting my heart broken.

Around eleven o'clock, while I was in kickboxing training, Bruno asked me if I could still meet him in the afternoon. I said, "Yes, I'm still down for it."

"Okay. I'll see you there at three o'clock," said Bruno.

After my kickboxing training, thirty minutes after one o'clock, I went home, showered, and got ready. I wore a black long-sleeved shirt, navy blue fitted jeans, and black knee-high boots. I didn't put any makeup on and didn't do my hair. Bruno was not someone I wanted to impress. Though I used dating apps, I didn't want to impress anybody during those times.

I had to take two buses to get to our meeting place, and I knew I was going to be late. I messaged Bruno on Instagram, saying, "Hey, I will be 15 minutes late. Are you there yet?"

"Yeah, I am right in front of the dental clinic. Walking in a circle."

I arrived fifteen minutes late and met him. I felt awkward when we finally met, and we both shivered in the cold. We hugged each other as a way of greeting. I never thought that he was more handsome in person than in the picture.

We strolled alongside the lake while having a conversation about various topics. During this time, I had the opportunity to discover more things about Bruno. He shared details about his occupation and interests.

Bruno was a skilled writer, writing poems and songs. He was also a construction worker and imported wine from Croatia to Canada. He was involved in other good activities, but I couldn't recall them all, as he had many responsibilities due to his hard-working nature.

We continued to exchange stories while walking; I found him to be very articulate and funny. I appreciated that he followed the sidewalk rule, walking closest to the road; it was one of the oldest acts of chivalry, and I liked him for that. I never thought I would like a man from southeastern Europe with curly blond hair and green eyes. His lips never got dry despite the cold weather and dry wind.

He sat on the bench by the lake, lit a cigarette, and said, "You can have a sit.".

"I'm okay. Thanks." I said nervously.

I didn't feel like sitting because I was cold, and I wanted to walk around to feel the heat in my body.

Around five o'clock in the afternoon, we went to the restaurant near the lake. Bruno managed to have a reservation of a table for six, so we had a lot of space, even though only the two of us were eating. The restaurant had bars, dim lights and alcohol displayed in the bar area. The tables in the restaurant were made of wood, or perhaps fake lumber, designed for the restaurant. We both took our jackets off and noticed Bruno had a lot of tattoos on his arms. I realized that I hadn't taken the time to check his Instagram account.

The server greeted us and gave us the menu brochure. I looked through the menu and wouldn't say I liked any of the foods they were serving.

I was trying to decide what I wanted to eat. Since I did kickboxing training, I thought of meat and wanted to fuel my body with protein. Ten minutes had passed, and I still couldn't decide what I wanted. Wine Rosé was my go-to drink but it was not available at the restaurant. Bruno suggested that we order a platter that we both could share. He had his drink, some whiskey with ginger ale. I had a light beer which was funny and awkward for getting a beer as a lady.

While waiting for our food to arrive, he told me about his first tattoo, a rose.

"It's about the song my dad wrote for my mom.". The rose tattoo on his arm was red and some shade of green and blue. He has another tattoo for his mom with "mom" inside the heart with a red and blue shade. He explained the meaning of every tattoo he had on his arms.

"The only thing I wouldn't get a tattoo for would be my wife."

'So, you won't get a tattoo for me?' I thought.

"Oh yeah, that makes sense," I said. I only had a few words to say.

'He loves his mom for getting her tattoos.' I thought.

He let me take a sip from his drink. "You can try my drink," said Bruno.

"Do you have STD or herpes?" I asked him jokingly before sipping from his drink.

"No." he answered sharply and shook his head. He probably felt weird about me asking him if he had STD or herpes.

Bruno talked about his country, its culture, and its food. He asked me if I had ever tried Ćevapi (Balkan Sausage).

"No, I never tried that," I said. He knew how to stir up conversation. He always looked into my eyes as if he could see my soul, and I wasn't used to making eye contact.

When our food arrived, I took a picture of it. I took the pork ribs from our platter and used utensils to eat them. "You can use your hands to eat them, haha, you don't have to use a fork." Bruno said.

"It's okay; I don't wanna get my fingers dirty," I said.

"There's a washroom you can wash your hands after." He insisted.

"It's okay," I politely declined.

"What is your favourite movie?" he stirred up topics we could talk about once again.

I looked at him in my shyness. The mesmerizing beauty of his green eyes and warm smile captivated me, leading me to introspection and wonder. I paused momentarily and said, "It's a Thai movie, and I forgot what it's called."

"What is it about?" he asked.

"I can't remember." My heart beat faster, my hands sweat, and I avoided eye contact. I took a bite of the biscuit from the platter like a robot, stiffed.

Bruno checked his phone, and I saw that he was shocked by my answer because I did not remember my favourite movie and what it was about. I couldn't talk properly as I was getting dizzy with a light beer. There was buzzing in my head, and I had to take a deep breath. I was starting to feel lightweight, and I wasn't used to drinking alcohol. I asked the waiter to serve more water.

"What is your favourite song?" he asked another question, seemingly not satisfied with my answer about my favourite movie that I totally forgot.

"My Heart Will Go On by Celine Dion. It's from the Titanic movie." I felt a bit relieved I was able to answer with a specification this time.

"Oh, that! What is your favourite song in your language?" he asks me again.

I couldn't think of any Filipino songs then since I had been listening to English love songs and random rap songs while working out. I scanned the restaurant, thinking about what Filipino song I used to like, and then I thought about the Filipino singer, one of my favourites, Bugoy Drillon. Then I searched for his name and played the song called "Muli," which translates to "Again, once more, and repeated." It's a song about taking another chance to be together again with an old love.

"So, you like slow songs?" He asked me. "Yes." I smiled.

He took a pork rib from the plate and ate. I couldn't think of questions I could ask him.

We talked a lot, but he mostly took the lead in our conversation because I didn't know what else to say. I didn't have many life experiences like him. He was four years older than me, and I barely went outside to hang out and explore the world. I also realized that I was the boring one, not Bruno. I was impressed by Bruno's passion when he talked about his culture and family.

"Where do you wanna go after this?" I asked him.

"Home. We could walk for a bit."

"Okay, I'll probably take the bus after we walk," I said.

"I'm not gonna let you take the bus alone." He shook his head as he looked into my eyes. He sounded calm and manly. As I looked into his eyes, I felt a moment of stillness wash over me as I searched for the right words to respond. My voice was soft but resolute when I finally spoke: "Okay, thank you."

He paid for our dinner. We had some leftovers, which he asked to be wrapped up so he could take them home.

We left the restaurant and took a moment to walk by the lake slowly. Bruno made me feel that I needed to calm down.

I used to be in a rush mode. I worked at fast food restaurants for many years since I was a teenager, where taking things slow was impossible, and I didn't have time to relax my mind. I had to walk fast to catch the bus, and I had to move faster at work. That is what I'm accustomed to. At work, I had to move quicker and take the customer's orders in a second. If not, the customer would be yelling and complaining. That was the life that I was used to. Bruno just expressed a new wave of calmness towards me, entirely different from the vast, rushing waves I always experience as a fast-food worker. Meeting Bruno calmed me down from the inside.

My favourite part of our date was walking by the lake. We weren't in a rush, and for the first time, I felt I had so much time in the world. Bruno made me think that it was okay to sit down and relax, and I didn't have to walk faster when I didn't want to.

We were about to call an Uber, and I asked him how his day with me was. I was chewing gum and looking for a trash bin to spit my gum, but I couldn't find any.

"Well, my day will not be completed without a kiss," Bruno said.

I didn't expect him to say that. That made me blush, and my heart melted. I was too shy to respond and didn't know if I should kiss him. I felt a bit panicky inside!

'Why did he ask me for a kiss? Did he like me? Is it a goodbye kiss forever? A goodnight kiss? Is this the kind of culture he grew up in?' I thought.

We walked towards the lake once more and sat on the cement seat. I was not ready for a kiss. I knew I liked him, and my heart grew fond of him as I got to know him.

"No." I was not ready and was shy about the kiss that he asked for.

Bruno called for our Uber, putting my address first and then his. We then went to the other side of the road and waited for two minutes for our Uber. We talked for a bit, and then we saw the white car.

"That's our Uber," he said.

We looked at each other. The world around us seemed to disappear as we stood on the sidewalk. Our eyes locked in a moment of connection and anticipation. Slowly, we leaned towards each other, our bodies pressing together perfectly. His gaze dropped to my lips, and before I knew it, our mouths had met in a tender, passionate kiss. It was a kiss that sent shivers down my spine and made my heart skip a beat. The softness of his lips was unlike anything I had ever experienced, and I knew then that I would never forget that magical kiss.

He opened the door for me. We got into the white car, and the Uber drove off.

In the car, we held hands and kissed once more. Then he realized we had forgotten the food to be taken out and left it at the restaurant! We couldn't cancel the Uber or return to the restaurant. I felt bad. I hadn't noticed that he wasn't carrying the leftover food from the restaurant.

Before I got dropped off, we kissed each other goodbye. I remember how I felt as I closed the car door and entered my house. My heart jumped for joy, and for a moment, I couldn't stop smiling. I got a text from him saying that he had a great time with me and thanked me for going out with him. We both thanked each other for our time on text message and said a good night text.

Two days after our date, he only messaged me once after I messaged him first. I knew he didn't like me because nothing had come out of my mouth during the date, but I liked him. We talked once in a while, and he asked me out again, but since my fast-food job didn't give a schedule in advance, I couldn't decide if I would be available to see him again.

"I don't know yet; I'm busy with work," I replied to Bruno's invitation.

He asked me a few more times if we could meet, and I gave him excuses that I was swamped with my two jobs. Technically, I turned him down every time he asked me.

4

LIFE UNEXPECTEDLY

I got into a snowboarding accident in the first week of March 2020. I got a mild concussion. I had to take a break from my two jobs for a week. My family physician advised me to stay home, relax, eat healthy foods, take vitamins, and not exercise, not to go to work. I wasn't allowed to listen to music, writing, using my phone, and watching the television. For one week, I was not allowed to go outside and use my phone. I had to tell Bruno I wouldn't be able to see him that weekend, but we could meet the weekend after and when I finally feeling well.

After one week, I felt better. I opened my phone immediately to catch up with people; it was the 11th of March 2020, and the lockdown started. I received a message from Bruno that was sent on the 10th of March 2020, saying, "Hey, I just wanted to ask if you're free this weekend and if you're feeling better."

Then I replied, "Hey, I'm okay now, but I can still feel my head hurt slightly. Thanks for asking. I'll let you know later tonight if I'm free this weekend."

"Okay." he said. Six hours later, he messaged me again and said, "I made plans for the weekend, and I'm also not gonna ask you out anymore."

"Oh, why not?" I asked.

"Cause it's been over a month I've asked you countless times. You shut me down every time."

His reply shattered my heart.

"I'm sorry. I can't divide my time, and I am still waiting for my manager to change my schedule. I asked them to give me the weekend off. If that's your decision not to ask me out anymore, I respect that. It's my fault." I reasoned out. I read his message twice, and my heart sank like a stone in water.

Bruno reached his limitations, which made me feel guilty for rejecting him. At that time, I was young and inexperienced. I didn't have any idea how to share fun moments with him. Bruno mostly talked about himself and his amusing moments with his friends, while I had barely explored life outside my comfort zone.

I regret turning him down. My insecurities and lack of confidence swallowed me up, and I lost my chance to speak with an attractive man like him again. I felt he was too good to be true, and I knew he wouldn't be mine. Looking back, I realized that my hostile attitude towards life prevented me from making meaningful memories and connections—and above all, a connection to someone who could possibly be the one for me.

A week later, he asked when we were meeting again. I felt happy yet scared of the news about the coronavirus spreading quickly.

"When the coronavirus is gone," I said.

"That's a long time." He said.

I felt hopeless in our situation because we weren't allowed to meet anyone unless it was essential and necessary. Bruno stayed at his job since he was a construction worker, and I stayed on both of my jobs since I was working at a fast food restaurant. My other job became an online job where I Facetime my boss, who sent me tasks I could do on my work laptop at home. The world has shut down, closing any "unnecessary" businesses and only opening the essentials, such as grocery stores and fast-food restaurants; the construction and transportation workers were essential during the pandemic. I realized that time that life happens when least expected. I thought the coronavirus wouldn't reach Canada, yet it reached the world.

5

13TH MARCH 2020

As a cashier at a fast-food restaurant, I didn't know whether to wear a mask or not, but I wore it anyway. Although it was weird and itchy on my face, I told myself, *'I ain't gon catch the virus.'*

I walked down to the bus stop on my way to work, and I could still feel my skull pinching through my head due to a snowboarding accident early in March 2020. I knew I could work since I took a week off from moving too much. I usually use my headphones to listen to music while commuting to work, but I forgot my headphones that day. I was alone with my thoughts. I might or may not lose my job at fast-food since I was not done with my probation month, and they may want to keep people who had been working there for a while. There was a total of uncertainty regarding my job.

Crossing the road, I pressed the call button for the white silhouette to appear and safely cross the pedestrian. I couldn't help but notice the atmosphere on the road; it was lonely. The garbage bins beside the bus stop were full, and the lids were barely closed, as if no one had pulled the garbage bins out in weeks. I could easily jaywalk on the road and didn't have to check left to right to see if a car was coming my way. That was how empty the road was when we had a lockdown.

I saw a couple of cars, and I could also see the drivers wearing surgical masks and disposable gloves while driving. It looked like we were living in an apocalypse. This reminded me of the book I read in high school,

"The Road," by Cormac McCarty. The book is about the unnamed father and son travelling to safety as an apocalypse wipes out the Earth.

It was 10 degrees Celsius. I wore my work uniform, a sweater, and a winter jacket. While waiting for the bus to arrive, I could hear empty cans rattling on the sidewalk as the wind blew. Some ripped plastic bags and old newspapers flew up to the trees. I couldn't smell anything but mint chewing gum from my mouth while wearing a mask.

I checked my social media as I sat at the bus stop seats. Scrolling through social media during the pandemic was both depressing and funny. It was heartbreaking because of the lockdown and reading some stories of the people who caught the virus, had a hard time catching their breath, and didn't know whether they would survive. It was also funny that some people would make jokes out of the pandemic situation and make memes out of the COVID-19 pandemic. It gave me a bunch of laughs during the pandemic.

Scott sent me a voice message copying the iconic Cardi B voice "cooroownaviraaasss.". I laughed my arse off alone at the bus stop. Hearing his voice sounded like a male version of Cardi B's voice.

I also checked some of my friends on social media while waiting for the bus to arrive. I noticed that some of them who were supposed to graduate in 2020 labelled their bio on Instagram as "quarantined '20" since they were supposed to graduate in March 2020, and some of them were supposed to graduate in June 2020. Unfortunately, because of the pandemic, their graduation was postponed. I labelled my Instagram bio as "essential worker status" for fun.

As an essential worker, I took pride in going to work, but I was also afraid of catching and bringing the virus home. I lived with my mom, two brothers, and grandmother. I wanted to stay home during the pandemic, but I needed to continue working to pay for the phone bills, rent, and other necessities. I couldn't complain about needing to go to work during the lockdown.

When the bus arrived, the driver opened the front door and said, "you have to enter through the bus exit door". I entered through the bus exit door. There were signs on the bus such as "Maintain 2m distance", "Bus fare-free," and "Do not sit in this area." Some of the seats had black and yellow striped tape as a caution not to sit on designated bus seats to maintain social distancing. The bus driver only took five people in.

On the bus, I didn't want to think about having to go to work. I didn't want to expect anything at work. I was looking through the bus window, and I didn't see anyone walking on the sidewalk or a bunch of students going home after school. Weekdays were the usual busiest time, around three o'clock in the afternoon. It was odd not to see many high and middle school students laughing and cursing on the bus. Supposedly, the school March break starts on the 16th to the 20th of March 2020. But on the 13th of March 2020, they should be on the bus, perhaps noisier because of excitement for the upcoming break if the pandemic didn't happen. It used to bother me when the students were loud on the bus. But when the pandemic hit, there were no students in sight, the bus was silent, and all I could hear was an automated voice announcement at each bus stop.

When I got off the bus stop, I still waited for the pedestrian traffic light to turn red to white, and I followed the traffic lights despite not having cars around the area. It was dumb to do when I could cross the road since there was no traffic or cars on the road, but I was used to following the traffic light for pedestrians until it was my time to cross the road.

At my workplace, our store building has a huge parking lot right in front of it. The parking lot was empty that day; it used to be so busy since there was a gym, sports store, and food places beside my workplace. I could not believe it was happening, and seeing the empty parking lot made me think the world would end.

When I entered the store, there were no customers in sight. I barely knew the people working that day because I had only been working for almost two months. I wore my hairnet on my head, greeted my co-workers and went to the break room. I placed my bag on the table since the lockers were all occupied by my co-workers who worked early. I removed my mask since my co-workers weren't wearing masks. I felt awkward when I wore it. We weren't sure if we were supposed to wear the mask while working.

I went to the storefront, and the manager, Antonio, had an announcement: "Foods that you were getting for the break are now free, and we're going to buy bubble tea later. Thank you so much, everyone, for showing up."

Everyone cheered in excitement. I had never tried Bubble tea before that day and was excited to try it for the first time. For the first hour of my work, the store wasn't busy. All we did was clean the store and take customer orders if we had one. We didn't talk much about the virus. We were steady and waited for what the head office had to say about the protocols. So far, we just have to follow social distancing. We stopped giving buzzers we had used before the pandemic, as we might catch the virus from using them. The buzzers indicated that the customers' orders were ready for pickup.

The Bubble tea made me excited about taking orders. Antonio asked Jena to order the Bubble tea online, and she asked each one of us which flavours did we like for Bubble tea.

Antonio assigned me outside of the store that day. Once I took their orders, if they were small food items, we would make them right away, and if they were big orders, we would have to give them a waiting time. A few minutes later, Antonio called me and asked me to stay in the front store since there were no customers coming in.

Then, a customer came, wearing a shirt as if it was summer already, paired with tight jeans. I told him to stand behind the line, pointing to the green tape on the floor. He did as I said, but he looked pissed. I took his order, and when he was ready to pay, he extended his arms, handed the cash from where he stood, and said, "Is this what you want?" I didn't make rules or didn't mean to make the customer's life harder. I came near him to take the cash. He then took his order and left the store.

Another lady came in, wearing a mask and a face shield. She ordered a burger combo and asked, "Why aren't you wearing a mask? You guys are going to get sick!". Her eyes looked worried, yet so pissed by her forehead frowned. She mumbled again, and I couldn't understand what she said after she got her order.

I heard Antonio and other crew members laughing aloud in the kitchen area, and I walked toward Jena and asked about Bubble Tea. She said, "I accidentally put our home address, haha, instead of the store's. Sorry guys! But my mom will bring them here."

Jena accidentally put her home address as the delivery destination instead of our store's. We had to wait until Jena's mom came with Bubble tea.

6

ADAPTING TO NEW SAFETY PROTOCOLS

Adopting the "new normal" was nonsense to some people, but we didn't have COVID-19 vaccines back then, and we were not certain who was carrying the virus. We had to follow protocols that the government officials would implement. Seeing people with masks and face shields on was strange, but wearing a mask for myself was more bizarre. I was trying to learn how to breathe with a mask on because I was scared of catching the life-threatening virus, and it itched my face.

Fast-food establishments have to implement a range of safety measures to mitigate the spread of the virus. As fast-food workers, we must wear personal protective equipment (PPE) such as masks and gloves, practice frequent hand hygiene, and maintain physical distancing. While necessary, these protocols have added complexity to the job. We had to learn how to adapt to new routines quickly, ensuring our and customers' safety.

Our store's setup consisted of two cash registers, where we took all the orders, and people paid for them, with one cashier each. One or two people assembles the ordered items on the tray, and a person or two bagged the order and called the customer's name. One person was doing the online orders and phone call orders, but sometimes three people were doing them. Two people were assigned to the burger patty station, and two to three people were assigned to the frying station.

We put sanitizers on the counter and by the entrance door. We used to have buzzers that buzzed when customers' orders were ready, but we discontinued them due to the new normal. We also discontinued leaving plastic utensils by the counter for customers to take to prevent the spread of the virus. When our customers asked for more plastic utensils, we would have to give them to the customers while we wore newly worn gloves.

Our Manager, Antonio, had put a timer by the hand-washing sink to ensure we were washing our hands for 20 seconds since it was proper hand hygiene. We had to wash our hands regularly. They also provided gloves for us to wear while working; they were large and extra-large gloves, but we needed medium and small gloves. It was hard to wear large gloves because my hands were small, and the extra-large gloves would slide off my hands.

We were also coping with increased workloads. We implemented an online delivery order, which became in demand during the pandemic. We may not have customers inside the store or fewer customers than before the pandemic hit, but we've got a ton of online orders to prepare.

Before the lockdown, people could quickly enter our store, place an order, pay, and dine in or take out however they wished to. But during the pandemic, we had to change the entire setup of our store. People had to line outside the store, and we only limited and let six people inside. The government had strictly ruled that we had to stay apart or what we call "Social Distancing.". Our restaurant's management team had to put signs on the floor and outside the store that day. Signs and red circle stickers on the floor that say "Practice social distancing." Each red circle sticker was placed 6 feet apart in the line for customers and behind the counters to indicate a 6-foot distance.

"Hi there, how may I help you?" I greeted them with a little wave to the customer.

"Hi, before I order, can I ask you something?" said the customer.

"Yes, for sure!" I quickly responded.

"How can you only let six customers in while many of you work inside? It doesn't make sense. I see a lot of workers inside, and you only let six customers in. Oh, come on!" the customer seems frustrated with the "New Normal" routine that the fast-food restaurant implemented.

I took a deep breath. My head feels burning hot. Though she had the right to ask me that question, I didn't know how to answer politely then.

"uhm…" I said with a hesitation. I was thinking about what could be the best answer.

"We must follow the rules; it's just the protocol." that was the reply that just came out of me despite the many words I would like to say to the irritated customer. The customer was not happy with my response.

The customer responded with a shrill voice, "What the f*ck? Are you f*cking serious?"

I was stunned to speak. *'Should I call the supervisor?'* I looked at her and opened my mouth, but no words came. Then the customer said, "You know what? Just take my order! You guys are ridiculous!"

I took that customer's order. I hated that I didn't answer her in a way that the customer would understand better. Complaining about it made sense, but it was also hard for me to explain it to them. I knew what our store was working on about applying the new regular routine, but as of that day, it was hard to put them into words. I hadn't socialized with other people in a week due to a mild concussion, and I was trying to find the right words to say. I wish they wouldn't question us and follow our restaurant protocol. We were in a pandemic, and I just hoped people would understand.

We had to lock both entrance and exit doors so customers could only enter if we let them in. We were strictly following the rules the government had set up, even though some people may not want to agree and follow the protocols.

Then, it was quiet for some time, and Antonio asked me to come inside to the storefront and clean the trays. We could still take orders inside the store only if at most six customers were inside.

"I'm not used to this…" said Jeyja.

"Same! No customers in sight," Chase said as they threw the small fried chicken out. We didn't give our customers a small portion of chicken; we took them for a break or threw it out.

Another customer came to place an order. He looked like a handsome Asian with a mask on. He had straight black hair and deep-set eyes. He leaned on the counter, which was not allowed at the time. Green tape on the floor indicated they couldn't step further than the green tape line.

I greeted the customer and said, "Hi, can you please step backward behind the green line."

"Why?" the customer asked.

I paused for ten seconds before I answered him, "We have to follow the rules, and we should stay 6 feet apart".

Then he said, "why? That's stupid."

I didn't know how to answer his 'Why?' question, so I said, "I know it's stupid, but it's in the news that we have to follow the new normal."

I honestly have had the worst explanation to the customer. I haven't fully understood why we had to do all that because I was also one of them; I was like them, just a person trying to navigate life through the new normal like everybody else. Hence, my struggle to explain something I was not yet fully aware of, just like the rest of the world.

"Why?" he inquired again, looking clueless about the rule I just said about social distancing.

Perhaps he was trying to piss me off, and he got on my nerves. If hitting them with the trays was legal, I have done it already. He might be handsome, but I wished he would watch the news more.

"Can I just take your order?" I said.

He leaned against the counter, which pissed me off!

"Sir, can you please stand behind the line? You are not allowed to stand near me." I sternly warned him.

"Oh, f*ck off!" He shouted and left. He pushed the doors with all his might. My heart beat faster, and my hands were shaking. My co-workers looked at me as if I had been convicted of stealing or doing something wrong to the customer. *'Was it my fault that I raised my voice slightly because it was hard to talk while wearing a mask?'* I raised my voice just in case he didn't hear what I said.

My co-worker Sheena came to me and said, "He's handsome but doesn't watch the news."

About 5–8 people, including a supervisor, worked in the kitchen. Some of my colleagues quit because of the pandemic, and some found another job. At the storefront where I worked, some cashiers also packed orders. We still received many orders through online delivery during the pandemic, and obviously, we needed as many people to work as possible, even during that time.

I preferred doing the online delivery even though it got busy most of the time since I didn't want to talk to people in person. Most customers I served at the storefront would ask about the protocols and why they had to wear a mask upon entering. I was fed up trying to explain the protocols to the customers. I was tired of repeating myself whenever customers asked why they needed to wait for a long time outside and why we only let six people in. I know how hard it was to wait outside in the cold, but we, as fast-food workers, were helpless, too. As much as we didn't want to adjust to the "new normal," we had to follow the rules of 6 feet apart, the need to wear masks upon entering the store, and only one person who was allowed to order if a family was ordering food.

As the pandemic forced many restaurants to close or limit their operations, fast-food establishments experienced a surge in demand. We used to operate until midnight, finishing cleaning the store by 2:00 or after midnight. Then, suddenly, when the pandemic occurred, we changed our operating time from 8:00 to 22:00, from Monday to Sunday.

With fewer options, fast-food workers handled larger orders, often with reduced staff due to burnout, safety protocols and health issues. This increased workload placed additional strain on workers, both physically and mentally. Despite the challenges, we remained dedicated to providing quality service, even when exhausted.

7

THE PAUSE

I started working at that fast-food restaurant pre-COVID period. Tons of people come into our store which makes it crowded as always. Some days, we had to ask groups of people who wanted to dine in to wait an hour to two hours because there weren't enough tables available.

I remember having seven groups of family come in to dine with us, and some of them sang the Happy Birthday song loudly and asked us if we could play a "Happy Birthday" song, but we didn't have that kind of service in our store, and we couldn't change the music that's being played. People were more friendly and enthusiastic back then.

Since the lockdown began in March 2020, I have started making friends at work. I thought that I needed to loosen up a bit since I had to stay working at the fast-food restaurant for a while until the pandemic ended.

I made friends with people who trained me at work especially Chase and Jeyja. I became close with Chase first since we both worked together every day in the afternoon.

"How old are you?" Chase asked.

"I'm twenty one." I replied.

"No way!" Chase teased me, not believing what I just said about my age.

"Haha! Why? How old are you?" I returned his question to him.

"I'm twenty one too, girl! We're the same age!" said Chase excitedly. "I never worked with someone with the same age as me. They're either older or younger than me."

"Right? I'm glad we're the same age and like, we can understand each other more." I told Chase.

"Right?"

Chase was just like me; we were both still figuring out what life had to offer. I didn't know how young we were in our early twenties, and I thought it was beautiful not knowing what we wanted to do in life so that we could try a few new things.

I told Chase about Bruno and the people I've dated. Chase shared the same thing they had also gone through. We shared our heartbreak stories, love life secrets, dreams and everything we could imagine sharing about our lives. I felt safe when Chase was there; we instantly became "work besties." Besides Chase, I met Jeyja. Jeyja taught me a lot at work, and we got along well. She is younger than Chase and me.

⇩⇩⇩

It was bizarre not to see many customers at the store when the pandemic hit. Though we get through online transactions and call & pick up orders, I wasn't used to seeing fewer people coming in on our store. The call & pick-up orders were for customers who placed them over the phone and were picked up at a specific given time by the worker who took the order. We would give them a waiting time to pick up. Some of my co-workers were assigned to both online transactions and taking call orders.

I was primarily assigned to online transactions and call-and-pick-up orders. I barely take orders outside, but I mainly cover for my co-workers who will take their break from outside order taking.

We had two phones so we could take orders as fast as possible. But sometimes, only one person was assigned to take calls and online orders.

"Hello, good afternoon, welcome to our store. How may I help you?" I said over the phone.

As I took the customer's order over the phone, the other phone rang.

"Hello? I cannot hear you." she said.

"Hello, what can I get for you?" I said.

"Can I get a drink? Hello? I can't hear you properly" She said.

"Sorry, which drink would you like?" I repeated my question.

"Can you turn off the phone ringing because it hurts my ear and I can't hear you properly."

I didn't respond; I couldn't just end the call on the other line. In the back of my head, I said, *'You should be grateful that I am taking your orders and not these people who are waiting for their calls to be answered.'* I wish I could say that and be rude to the customer at least twice daily. But of course, I wouldn't do that. I couldn't just do that.

"I am going to repeat the order!" The customer said harshly.

As she repeated her order, the other phone rang again. She got irritated and said, "It is disrespectful to me that there is a phone ringing over my ear, and we both can't hear each other. I am going to the store and add some more. This is ridiculous. Your style of taking orders is beyond disgraceful!"

"Okay, can I take your name?" I asked her calmly; then the phone rang again.

"Say that again!" she roared in anger which hurt my ear.

I kept putting the other phone on silent mode and asked her name again. I told her it would take 15 minutes for her order to be ready. She hung up the phone when I told her about her waiting time. I tried to turn the other phone in silent mode but the phone would still ring loudly.

After taking the lady's order over the phone, the phone rang again. The phone was ringing non-stop that I also want to take a break too like my co-workers.

I went to the dine-in area to see through the window glass how long the line was outside. One of the customers inside the store's line approached me and said, "Hi." She almost touched my arm with her bare hand. I stepped back from her.

She said, "I'm calling the store right now and there's a lot of people working but nobody answers the phone."

Then I said, "We get a lot of calls every day, but keep calling."

'Why do you need to call the store, woman? You're already inside, and it just added to the noise.' I thought.

I went to the break room as fast as I could. I was hungry and needed to fuel my body for another three hours of work, but I stayed in the breakroom for ten minutes because I didn't want to see the lady who asked me about us not answering her call.

Chase covered me for calls and online orders. After ten minutes, I went to the front and took two fried chicken, mashed potatoes, and soda. Chase prepared my food for me and placed an extra scoop for my mashed potatoes.

"Yay! Thanks!" I express my happiness at Chase's kind gesture.

Sometimes, I bring my lunch but usually take food from our store. There were limited foods we could get for free, but we got a 50% discount on food for our lunch, and we were not supposed to make our own food. We must punch them in on the cash register with the supervisor code, and our co-workers must complete the food for us. I didn't mind paying for 50% discounted food since I got to choose which part of the chicken I wanted, and I could get the newly cooked chicken.

While eating my food in the breakroom, it was hard to resist not to use my phone because I didn't know much about my co-workers. It was awkward to start a conversation mainly if I ate with a co-worker who works in the kitchen or the fry area.

As I was scrolling through my social media and eating the fried chicken, I saw lots of friends on Facebook who had started reading books they hadn't read before. They could finish reading books since they had nothing to do during the lockdown. Some were forced to stay home without work and no income. Some were given the option to work from the comforts of their home.

The general public has no other option but to stay in their home, social media is one of the most popular ways to be entertained, to be updated regarding the virus or discover new recipe that one can make from home. One recipe that went viral during the pandemic was the whipped coffee called "Dalgona coffee."

I never had the chance to make that viral coffee recipe since I worked a lot. People started new hobbies such as crocheting stitches, painting, drawing and reading. I wish I could stay home and try those things as well. I realized that we may live in the same world, but our lives are entirely different. Anyhow, I should not compare myself to others, especially those I see on social media, because, for sure, just like me, there are many things that are happening that we don't share on social media.

We had no pending orders when I finished my break and went to the storefront.

"Wow! All finished?" I was amazed by my co-workers.

All orders were made for online delivery; we just had to wait for the drivers to pick them up. We didn't have any call-and-pick-up orders for a good hour.

"Yeah! When you were gone, everyone picked up the speed and was fast. Hahaha" Rolland said jokingly.

"Shut up, *Kalbo*," I said laughingly.

Jeyja and Chase died of laughter because they got the inside joke. Rolland was telling me that everyone was fast at the store when I was not there working.

We cleaned the store and stocked up what we needed in the front. Our manager, Antonio, sent some people home who had started early and whoever wanted to go home. Most people in the back wanted to go home. One of my co-workers, whom I had never had a chance to get his name since he quit by the end of March 2020, said, "Can I go home and still get paid?" and everyone laughed at what he had just said. Everyone laughed at small things and even the weirdest joke my co-workers would crack. Antonio didn't let him go because we still needed him to work.

As I was wiping the front counter, I realized that seeing only a few people in our store was also an excellent moment. It was good to pause. It was great hearing only your co-workers laughing and talking loudly; not many customers coming in. It was hard to adopt the new normal because we had to stay 6 feet apart. However, there was peace from the disturbance within me.

Finding time to relax and take a break can be challenging in a fast-paced world. However, during the first wave of the pandemic, I came to appreciate the value of pause. I learned how to slow down and take some time to reflect because I met great people like Chase and Jeyja when things slowed down. The year 2020 compelled us to slow down and taught us to value the opportunity to take a break.

8

CUSTOMER'S EXCUSES

Some people were not wearing masks due to medical reasons. Those unable to wear masks should provide a doctor's note stating that they were an exception to a mask policy. As of June 2020, it had been three months since the lockdown. It's been three months of news about the coronavirus, and they were everywhere on social media. Everyone is expected to know about the mask policy, and I assumed everyone on Earth knew about it.

Some customers come in without a mask despite the signs on the entrance door and window glass stating that they must wear one upon entering. Our restaurant policy was that everyone who entered the store building should wear a mask.

I, as a fast-food worker and the rest of the team didn't want to wear masks either. We were wearing masks because we were protecting ourselves. People who entered the store without a mask didn't know how hard it was to continuously and politely remind the customers to wear masks.

What was most annoying was that, when a customer said they were an exception to the mask policy, they couldn't provide a doctor's note or proof stating they could not wear a mask. Out of 100% of the customers, 70% wore a mask, and 30% claimed they were exceptions to the mask policy and said they were coming back to show me proof, but they never returned. I usually worked at the cash register and online delivery orders; I worked almost every day with just one day off. But I have never seen a doctor's note or any medical note that a person is exceptional for mask policy. Perhaps they were lying and didn't want to wear a mask. I know some of our customers would go to a store where they sell masks before coming to our restaurant to buy food, while others didn't care.

One of our supervisors said, "If an auditor caught our store with customers without masks, our store was prone to closing down." But for some people who didn't want to wear masks, we just let them go instead of arguing with them. We were all tired and didn't have the energy to argue with them.

The hardest part of our job as cashiers was when a customer wasn't wearing a mask. We would get in trouble for that, and the supervisors would talk to us.

A customer came in without a mask, and Rolland said from the kitchen,

"Rainna, why is the customer not wearing a mask?"

"He said he had a doctor's note and would come back," I replied.

"Why did you let him in without a mask? What if he's carrying the virus?" Rolland said.

I felt hopeless when a conversation started with, 'Why is that customer not wearing a mask?'

'Why didn't he ask the customer? He's the supervisor,' I thought. *'It was dumb to ask a cashier why the customer isn't wearing a mask.'*

"He said he's gonna come back and show the doctor's note." I reassured him.

I felt the audacity to answer the supervisor loudly, taking short breaths in each sentence. I was irritated by Rolland. I understand it was our job to inform the customers about our mask policy, but supervisors shouldn't get the crew members into trouble if they don't want to wear masks.

BEHIND THE PLEXIGLASS

Our supervisors put a lot of weight on our shoulders instead of throwing a bone to make our job easier. Everyone was going through different things in life that were weighing them down, and crew workers like us were not exempt from that. I hope that instead of putting us down, our supervisor helped us instead.

☙❧☙

When we opened some dining tables, a man came to our store without a mask.

"Hi, sir, you need to wear a mask upon entering our store," I informed him calmly. He was staring at me as if I said something terrible.

"I cannot serve you if you aren't wearing a mask," I warned him. His forehead furrowed and said, "I can't wear a mask, and I can't breathe with a mask on."

'Neither do I, sir. I can't breathe properly with a mask on. But I have to.' I thought.

Rolland yelled, "The mask, Rainna!" I ignored Rolland and continued serving the customer without a mask. He ordered a few burger combos.

"It's gonna be ten minutes for your order." I told the customer.

"Okay. I'll come back, " he replied, leaving the store.

"Rainna, don't forget the mask policy." Rolland reminded me the second time. I ignored him again. I knew what I was doing, but I was helpless. I could not force our customers to wear masks if they didn't want to.

The customer, without a mask, came back after fifteen minutes. He came with a face shield on, then asked one of my co-workers, Lester, who was bagging the order and said, "Hi, I ordered this." he showed his receipt to Lester.

"Rolland, how long is the next chicken?" Lester asked Rolland.

"Twenty minutes. They're still breading." Rolland said. My heart sank, and I felt uneasy. I had a gut feeling that the customer would get mad at us. Then the customer said, "I needed to wait for another twenty minutes? Are you serious? That's bullsh*t!"

"We didn't have enough chicken. I'm sorry," I said.

The customer took off his face shield and said, "How long should I wait until? Is this a fast food?".

"Rolland, can you talk to the customer?" I approached Rolland.

Rolland slammed the trays on the counter in the back and walked up to the customer.

I couldn't handle any more negativity and complaints. I had enough for the day. Taking long list of orders, I barely drank water and couldn't go to the washroom. I was burned out. Rolland resolved the problem, and the customer waited.

I took the order from our last customer in the line, and he was okay with waiting. I asked Rolland, who was having a temper if I could go to the washroom quickly, but he ignored me. I asked the other supervisor, Adrianna, and she said, "Okay, be quick." I went to the crew washroom, but someone was inside. My three co-workers were waiting as well. We weren't allowed to use the customer washrooms because they were closed for us and the customers to use.

I sat in the chair to wait. The other two workers were chatting about their lives. After a few minutes, I finally drank water, and my co-workers said I could use the washroom first and they could wait for me. I felt light-hearted for my co-workers, who were nice and gentlemanly. I used the washroom quickly, then returned to the storefront.

9

THE VIRUS WAS SCARED OF HIM

On a dreary Monday afternoon, as the rain poured outside, a disgruntled customer expressed frustration about waiting an extended time.

A customer approached the counter, removed his mask, and said angrily, "How long will it take for my order? I need to go!" Everyone around him looked at this particular guy. Rolland looked sharply through the hot shelves and carefully listened to the customer's complaint.

'Well, another customer complained. What's new anyway?' I thought.

That was my usual thought when a customer was complaining. This was just one of many complaints we receive daily; even the most minor issues, such as forgetting to give the customers a few pockets of ketchup, are regularly brought to our attention.

The customer was about 5'10 feet tall, 210 lbs and probably in his 50s. He looked aggressive and placed his knuckles on the counter. *'Why can't he wait for only 10 minutes?'* I thought. I was at fault for not letting the customer know we'd had a waiting time for the chicken.

We had many customers since we were one of the essentials during the pandemic. I understood the customer's frustration for waiting a long time, but we tried our best to accommodate and assemble orders as much as possible and as fast as we could. The fried chicken takes 20 minutes to cook in a deep fryer. We needed to be in control of making the chicken faster, but we could not do it more quickly.

Rolland approached the customer and said, "Almost done, sir."

"I've been waiting here for a long time!" the customer replied.

"We will do your order immediately." Rolland reassured the customer and returned to the kitchen. The customer still mumbled some words and leaned to the counter which was not allowed during the pandemic.

About four customers behind him were waiting and looking at him. They were standing 6 feet apart at the "pick-up order" line. I was scared that he would come to me and complain. I took his order and forgot I had to tell him he needed to wait for a while. It was my responsibility to let the customers know how long it would take for their orders to arrive, but I neglected my responsibility.

The man still waited for his order, not wearing his mask. He looked as if he was not scared of the virus.

One of my co-workers whispered, "The virus is scared of him."

We laughed silently. After twelve minutes, the chicken was up and ready.

"*Ateng*, do his order first so he can get out," Rolland said.

He would call me "*Ateng*" or any other name but my name. "Ate" (a-te) in Tagalog (Filipino language) means older sister or a respectful way to call a female person. Rolland added the word "ng" to "ate" to make it sound funny since he was older than me. We immediately prepared and gave the customer's order since he was not wearing a mask, and we needed to let him out immediately. The other customers took their orders, said nothing, and left the store.

10

OUT OF KETCHUP

I was assigned to take orders during the bustling afternoon shift, where the restaurant was filled with the lively chatter of customers wearing masks and the enticing aroma of fried chicken and freshly prepared burger patties. Rebecca bagged the food items while Chase and Bill assembled the orders. There were about ten people in the line. Macy was doing online orders and picking up the phone to place the orders.

I adjusted my mask and face shield as I took a customer's order wearing dark purple eye shadow, black eyeliners, and fake lashes. *'She must have been wearing full makeup under her disposable mask,'* I thought. Her eyebrows were delicate, arched on the point, and looked like a checkmark. She didn't have to wait long to get her order, as she only ordered a piece of chicken, mashed potatoes, and a drink, which were available then. We had it ready for only two minutes.

When the lady got her order, I took about ten trays from the counter to put them in their place. She asked for ketchup, and I answered, "I am so sorry; we ran out of ketchup," as I held the trays.

She got irritated. I noticed she held her car keys tightly and her forehead furrowed.

Then she said, "You know what? This is the only restaurant that does not have ketchup. How can you sell fried chicken without ketchup?"

'Chicken doesn't go with a ketchup, woman.' I thought.

I apologized and said, "I'm sorry; we didn't get the deliveries yet. We give out gravy for the chicken orders, and you have small gravy in the bag."

She left the store, stomping as she walked out and had difficulty opening the door because of the wind. Some new customers came in, and one of my co-workers came to take their orders. I walked out. I needed to take a break; I wouldn't say I liked complaints like that. I wanted to answer her rudely. I wanted to tell her to go to the restaurant that has ketchup, but there were better things to do.

I slammed the trays. Rebecca, who was bagging orders, asked me if I was okay. I took a deep breath and sighed as I bit my lower lip. I almost burst into tears. My forehead felt intense as I looked at Rebecca.

"No, I am not! The customer was like, 'This is the only restaurant that doesn't have ketchup!'" I told Rebecca, mimicking the customer's voice.

"As if this was the only restaurant that did not run out of ketchup!" My voice was louder than usual.

"Oh, what the f*ck! She should go somewhere else or buy a whole ketchup next door!" Rebecca retorted.

Bill said, "But we give gravy."

"Exactly! I was like, we give gravy for chicken orders. It's so annoying." Agreeing to Bill.

I loved how my co-workers joined me when I was angry at the customer. I felt I was not alone, and they felt the same frustration as I had. We were open every single day, and despite the lockdown, we had a lot of customers coming in once in a while; of course, we would run out of things in our store because we didn't get deliveries every day—we only got deliveries once or twice a week.

I felt so heavy in my chest that I almost wanted to cry because I got annoyed. I felt terrible that I could not fight with the customer, and all I could do was slam the trays over the counter as I talked to Rebecca.

Deep inside, I wished it rained and washed her face full of makeup. I expected something terrible would happen to her as she walked out of the store for being rude and impatient.

I went to the break room to drink water. I was dehydrated from talking a lot to the customer and wearing a mask all day. I sat down as I drank water and checked my phone for two minutes.

I was blessed to have work friends like Rebecca, Chase, and Bill. Rebecca joined the fast-food restaurant a year after I joined. Like me, she had worked at another fast-food restaurant. She was a year younger than me. She knew exactly what to do with taking orders and bagging. We taught her some things, and it turned out that she was a fast learner.

Weeks passed, and Rebecca texted me that she was anxious about her life. I had no idea how she came up with those thoughts, and I had no idea what I did to make her feel comfortable with me so that she could start telling me her vulnerable feelings. But I said something to calm her down and gave her advice.

"I'm sorry you are going through it, Rebs, but it's gonna be okay, and you are beautiful." I encouraged her.

Since then, she has shared some vulnerable things towards me about herself. I also told her about my situation with Bruno.

"He manipulated me and lied to me for wanting me to be his wife and it broke my heart into pieces when he ghosted me for months." I said to Rebecca.

Rebecca said things that made me feel at ease. She knew how to put herself in someone else's shoes. Since then, both of us have become best friends.

When I left the break room, I thought, *'Round two for another enemy coming in.'*

When I reached the cash register, I was surprised to see a line and many people coming in. I politely told them to follow the signs on the floor indicating that the lines were 6 feet apart. Most of them had to line up outside.

"I'm sorry you have to go outside the store to wait." I informed the customers in the line.

They went outside, blocking the door. I told them nicely not to block the door and follow the lines horizontally on the sidewalk. We eventually put white tape on the sidewalk so that our customers would follow the social distancing protocol according to the lines on the sidewalk.

"Follow the lines, please," I said while pointing to the lines on the sidewalk that were 2 metres apart.

I felt bad for people who had to line outside the store, but because of our new policy, they had to wait outside, and we needed to follow the rules; otherwise, the head of management would close our store for not following the protocol.

I went inside and took the next customer in line. That customer was lovely. She understood the 'new normal' and respected us as workers. "Thank you for still working during the pandemic; it must have been hard for you guys." The lovely and understanding customer said. That melted my heart!

"Thank you so much! Not everyone appreciates us. Thank you!" I happily greeted her back.

Then I took the next customer. She had a big order. When she was ready to pay, I said, "You can tap or insert your card."

However, her card didn't go through three times, so she called her husband to get another card.

"I'm so sorry. My husband is coming in." She looks worried because her card has been declined.

"It's okay, take your time," I reassured her so she would not worry.

She was holding the line, and some customers were looking at me, waiting for me to take the next customer. One of my co-workers helped me. There were three cashiers in total.

Some days, I was okay with the customer taking so long to order because I could just take my time to daydream. Other times, I get irritated because of overwhelming customers and the need to take orders—that particular time, I wanted to take things slower. I didn't care how long I waited for this customer's husband to arrive.

"Wait, I am so sorry." the customer apologized again for making me wait.

"That's okay! I just want to let you know we don't have ketchup for your fries." I informed her about our lack of stock regarding the ketchup; I was hopeful that it wouldn't be an issue with her.

"Oh, no worries. We have a lot of ketchup at home." She said, squinting her eyes.

Their orders were ready at the counter because my other co-worker had done them while we were waiting for her husband.

Finally, the customer's husband arrived with a credit card, and it worked. They took their orders and said, "Thank you so much! I'm so sorry for the wait."

"No worries! Enjoy your meals!" I said, squinting my eyes. We squinted our eyes with a mask on, indicating we were smiling. Squinting our eyes was necessary because it was the only way to know we were smiling at them.

⁂

During the pandemic, we were considered one of the essential businesses. At first, it slowed down, but a few weeks later, many customers started coming in.

While we understood their frustration about waiting a long time to be lined up outside the store, we tried accommodating them and assembling their orders quickly. However, it took 20 minutes to cook the fried chicken in a deep fryer, and we needed to be in control of making it faster. Unfortunately, we were unable to speed up the process any further.

It got busy; many people lined up outside the store, and it started raining. Despite the social distancing protocol, my manager had to let the customers inside the store. I took the customer's order, which was next in line. The customer looked like she was in her 30s, she removed her mask as she spoke and told me about her orde. She was wearing red lipstick but not a mask.

"I'm gonna get a chicken, fries, and no drink." She said.

"I'm sorry, miss, but you must keep your mask on." I said.

She then put on a face shield without a mask. I saw she was wearing perfect red lipstick with a blue tone, and I wanted to compliment her. But I changed my mind. I feared she might not hear my voice through the mask, so I had to repeat myself so she could hear me complimenting her. I never liked repeating what I said because I was never talkative and spoke in a low tone.

"It would be twenty minutes to complete your order. Also, we don't have ketchup for your fries. Sorry about that." I said.

"Okay." she agreed and checked her phone with a purple and blue designed case.

We had to make another batch of fries and chicken because it was busy. The customers inside were all wearing masks, some with plastic face shields.

After five minutes of taking the order from the red lipstick lady, she went to the counter and said, "How long will it take for my order? I've been waiting for a long time!"

I was surprised because she was nice when I took her order. I told her there would be a waiting time, and I wanted to know about her red lipstick because it looked so beautiful.

After ten minutes, I gave her the order and said, "Here you go; I'm sorry about the long wait." She replied, "This is the slowest fast food I've ever been to. You gotta improve the service!"

I was hurt by what she said. I took it personally since I was working there, and telling me that it was the slowest restaurant made me feel I had bad customer service too.

I wished she would slip down or lose her red lipstick as she walked down the door.

I took a half-hour break and read some self-help books. Since I was not hungry, I drank water and read an electronic book. My mind was relaxed again, and I could do the following three more hours at my job.

As I walked to the storefront, I realized something. I didn't know where my thoughts were coming from. Perhaps it was from the books I had read or some deep thoughts. *'Does the rain have to do with my train of thought?'* I pondered.

I realized I might be happy for a short period if I saw that a short-tempered lady wearing red lipstick lost her red lipstick or that a full-makeup customer walked out and tripped on her way to the sidewalk. But would it change the fact that they made me feel little? I don't think so. I would be the one who would feel bad if something terrible happened to them. I would feel sorry if their bags were ripped off because then again, they would come back and complain for the second time around. They would complain about our plastic bags for not being sturdy enough. We would make their orders again because the food items would be all over the sidewalk or the parking lot. Not having a sturdy plastic bag would make our store look bad.

'That is not the point of life.' I thought. I realized then that I shouldn't wish anything bad on people.

Wishing something terrible to happen for someone who wronged me was not an answer that would benefit me. I sympathized with that lady with full-face makeup and the lady who wore adorable red lipstick. Perhaps they needed to go right away because their kids were waiting for them, and they needed to be there as soon as possible. Perhaps they needed to go to the hospital or somewhere urgent. Maybe they didn't mean to be rude. I was giving them the benefit of the doubt.

I didn't know who they were, and they didn't know me either, and that should rest the case. Deep inside, I am not a bad person who wishes ill for other people. Discovering that about myself after my encounter with those ladies made me a better person, and that's what matters.

11

SUNNY DAY

We had another setup at work in the summer of 2020. One Saturday morning, Antonio and other management staff had set up the new station, and they assigned me there to be the first worker to try it out. The management did everything to make our store faster and more efficient. They set up a new cashier near the entrance; we only had to take orders using that new station. Customers could only pay by card at that station; if they were paying by cash, they could pay at the storefront.

Most people didn't think about the seriousness of the COVID-19 pandemic because it was summer, and everyone wanted to enjoy a little sun. Most people I have noticed didn't wear masks. It was understandable that it was hot and sunny, and no one wanted to breathe through a mask. I saw a couple of people who were still wearing masks outside. I changed my disposable masks to washable masks because I could not breathe with the disposable ones, and it itched my face. The washable masks were soft on my face and didn't itch. I was given a new face shield that made me look like a cyborg wearing it.

"So, Rainna, I'm gonna assign you to the new station," said Antonio.

"Wow, we have a new station. I like it." I replied.

It was a little station near the entrance doors and the front store. It was located in the middle of the store. The new station had shelves and a long table. The phone was there, and a tablet to take orders in. When the new station wasn't busy, whoever was assigned to the new station had to cut the drink trays in half, take calls, and pick up orders. When the call and pick-up orders were ready, my co-workers would place the orders at the new station area.

A new customer came in and wasn't wearing a mask.

"Hi, sir. You have to wear a mask. I'm sorry," I told the customer who had just walked in.

"Oh, we still have to wear masks?" he asked.

"Yeah, I mean, the virus is still around," I replied, shrugging my shoulders.

"Okay, I'll just leave then." He said.

I then took the next customer's order.

"Hi there, how can I help you?" I said with a little wave.

"Wow! This is how we take orders now?" he said in amazement at our new station. I assumed this customer had been in our store before because he noticed our new station.

"Yes," I said noddingly, then continued, "but if you are paying with cash, you must go to the front. I can only take card payments here."

"Oh, okay, I'll pay cash." The customer said.

Then, the customer went to the front of the cash register, and my co-worker, Lester, took his orders, paid for his food, and said, "I'll be right back. I need to get something in my car."

Then, he walked to the exit.

Antonio caught and stopped him and said, "Sir, you have to exit to the main door; our exit door is closed."

"Oh, sorry." The customer said and went through the entrance doors to exit.

We had to close the exit doors because most people entered through the exit without wearing masks, and we had to control the line and the people coming in. We were strict with social distancing because we had to protect ourselves, too. I had to take extra precautions because my grandma lived in our house, and she had a weak immune system.

After an hour on my shift, it got busy.

"Rainna, go outside and take orders," said Antonio.

I had to take orders outside the store because there was a long line of customers. We let some people in to order at the new station inside the store, and Antonio took my place in the new station and took their orders. I had my tablet and laminated menu on hand and took the customer's order.

One customer asked, "Hi, are you guys open for dine-in?"

'Can you see people dining in? Dumbf*ck.' I said in my head.

My forehead felt intense, my nostrils flared, and my hands were sweating. I wanted to throw the sign at the customer for not reading them. We had two signs on both entrance and exit doors that said we were closed for dine-in and only taking online delivery orders, walk-in, and placing orders through phone calls with our store phone number; the signs were big enough for people to read them. We had a lineup outside the store, and this lady who asked if we were open for dine-in waited outside the store for a while. She didn't recognize the signs on the doors that were pasted on the window glass.

"No, we're not open for dine-ins yet," I replied to the customer's inquiry.

"Oh, okay. Do you know when you guys are opening for dine-in? My family wants to dine in." She said, and her forehead frowned.

"I have no idea. What can I get for you?" I asked abruptly.

The lady looked at the laminated menu I handed her. She spent minutes choosing what to order, then asked me again, "Is it okay to go inside? It's so hot here."

"No. We can't let you in unless your order is ready." I said.

The lady kept getting closer to me.

"Ma'am, can you please step backward for social distancing."

"Oh, sorry!" she said, backing up.

She still hasn't decided what to order. I tried to control my temper because that lady was getting under my skin.

A group of people were waiting outside the store, and I had to remind them to maintain a distance of two metres from each other, as indicated by the taped line on the floor. We placed tape on the sidewalk in front of our store and displayed a small menu on the window. We also had two laminated menus that we could hand out to the customers so they could decide what to order while they waited.

One of the customers asked if she could take the laminated menu home. In response, I informed her that the laminated menu was only meant for in-store use, but she could check the menu online anytime.

Another customer asked me, "Do we still need to wear a mask?"

'Can you see the people inside the store, outside, on the news, and me? Can't you see I'm still wearing a mask, face shield, and plastic gloves under the sun? Can you not see everyone around you that we're still wearing masks?' I said in my head.

I talked a lot in my mind because as much as I wanted to tell and cuss at the customers, but I didn't want to get in trouble, and it was a customer service job.

"Yeah, we still do," I said, turning to the lady who couldn't decide to order.

Then she got closer to me again and said, "Can I get the uhm…"

"Can you please back up?" I asked the lady.

'How many times do I have to tell you?' I thought.

The lady was about in her 40s. I judged our customers' age based on the way they ordered and the sound of their voices. Most young people, especially young adults, knew how to order. They mostly placed orders through online delivery and knew how to follow the protocols. Our adults and senior customers mostly had to be reminded to do social distancing and wear masks. We need to extend patience towards them because they think they know everything but don't know what they will order when they reach the cash register.

"I'm gonna get three burger combos." the lady finally ordered.

"Would you like cheese on your burger?" I asked her.

"What do you like?" She asked me back.

*'Am I going to eat what you're ordering? The f*ck?'* I said in my head.

"I..I don't know. I've never tried it." I said, lying.

I thought this would stop her questioning me, but I was wrong.

"You work here and never tried it?" she wondered.

I paused for a minute, looking at her face with a mask.

I raised my voice with wide-open eyes and said, "You're holding a lineup, ma'am. Do you still want to order? It's up to you if you want cheese on your burger."

I tried to hold my breath and sanity together and was shocked by what I said. It was my initial thought, but I let it out. I let it out, and it felt good in my chest.

She was shocked and screamed at me, "Okay, you know what? I'm not ordering!"

She tossed the laminated menu to the sidewalk and left. She stomped her feet, wearing dirty sleepers.

"That was so rude." The man in the line said.

I picked up the laminated menu and said to the man, "Yep. That's what I deal with every day."

I took the next customer's order, who was holding the other laminated menu. She ordered a few food items that we could prepare immediately, so I let her in.

"Just give me a second," I said.

'I don't like this job.' I thought.

I went inside the store, took the spray bottle with disinfectant, sprayed it on the laminated menus, and wiped it with a microfibre rug. I then went back outside and handed the menu to the next customer.

It was hot outside, and I felt like the sun was targeting me with its rays. I was sweating, dragged my legs outside the store to take the next customer without a mask, and craved a cold drink and some ice cream for refreshments.

When I finished work, I planned to go next door to get ice cream, but then I thought we had it at home. I left the store right after my shift was done. On the bus, I thought about the customer who tossed the laminated menu. I wish I could have said more about not being a robot worker. I get pissed too. I failed at work, too; I couldn't give good customer service if the customers were unwilling to cooperate. I was hurt. I was annoyed.

⇩⇩⇩

The next day, I was taking orders by the vestibule entrance door and told Antonio we had a lot of customers outside ready to take orders outside the store. I needed to communicate with whoever was working at the front and kitchen to let them know if they needed to make more food products.

"Okay, Rainna. Just finish taking orders, and you can go on your break. Are there any delivery orders? You can let them in," Antonio said.

"So far, none," I said.

A young couple came in while holding hands and without their masks on.

"Hi, welcome to fast food! I'm sorry, but you must wear your makas, and only one person can go in." I told them as they entered the store.

They immediately put their disposable masks on while giggling.

"We're not gonna get a lot." The lady said.

"Well, if you're not going to get a lot, then only one person can come in," I said firmly.

"I'm gonna get something," The man said.

"Okay, what can I get for you?" I asked the lady first.

"Why can't we go in together?" The lady said.

"It is our protocol. We are not allowed to let many people inside," I said, annoyed. "What can I get for you?"

I hated that she asked me that with an attitude as if she would get lost in the store if her boyfriend didn't come with her.

"I'm gonna get two burger combos, fries, and drinks. But for the fries, can I get them large?"

"Yep. Anything else?" I asked.

"Can I also get the soups you guys have?" She said.

"Yep. Anything else?" I asked.

"Actually, no soup, but I will get the three chickens, and one extra burger on the side and not combo," she said.

"Okay, will that be all?" I asked, hoping to finish the order taking.

"Yeah, that's it, I'll pay cash," she said.

"You can go to the front," I said, then I took the man's order, "and for you?"

"Can I just get a bottled water?" He said.

'Calm down,' I thought. I raised one eyebrow, looked at the customer's eyes firmly, and asked, "Anything else?"

"That's it." He answered.

'You've got to be kidding me?! You only wanted to get water, to be in our store and be with your girlfriend.' I thought.

"Okay, you have to wait outside since it's crowded right now," I said rudely.

The man was intelligent; he only ordered one item so he could come inside with her, but he didn't want to wait outside.

"I only ordered one bottled water," said he.

"Kay! Go to the front!" I said rudely.

There were about ten people inside the store, which was considered crowded. We weren't allowed to let many people in since we were taking precautions and trying to prevent the spread of the coronavirus.

'Why couldn't they split for like ten minutes?' I thought.

I understood it was a pandemic, and they probably hadn't seen each other. I had to take the next customer and repeatedly ask if they could dine at our store.

"No, I'm sorry. We are not open for dine-in," I said.

"Rainna, you can go on your break; Chase will cover you," Antonio said.

"Take a rest, girl!" Chase said, patting my shoulder.

"Thank you so much for saving my life!" I said.

Chase was more patient than I was; I didn't know how they handled taking customers and had to keep their minds sane. I ranted to Antonio about the young couple who didn't want to split up, and Antonio said, "Don't worry; they're going to break up soon."

We all laughed in the kitchen.

"They didn't get the water, though. They cancelled it. They said they didn't need it," Jeyja said.

"Wait, what? They outsmart us!" I exclaimed. I had felt the heat in my body. "I told them only one person can come in, and the guy ordered bottled water, and they didn't get it?"

"Yeah, they didn't. So annoying!" Jeyja exclaimed.

12

UNCONTROLLED BEHAVIOUR

One day, I was on my break, and as I waited for my food order, I stood at the corner where we make delivery orders; I heard a customer yelling at my co-worker, Jeyja.

Once we cashed out the order, two receipts came out after the order transaction had been done. One copy of the receipt was for the customer, and the other was for us to check the food item ordered. We would give the receipt to the person assembling the food order. As we put the food order on the tray, we would put a checkmark on each item on the receipt copy to ensure the order was accurate.

Jeyja checked the receipts, both the customers' and ours and found that everything the customer paid for was in a plastic bag.

"Everything is in the bag, ma'am, and we double-checked them," said Jeyja, reassuring the angry customer.

However, the customer insisted that she ordered two items not on the receipt, meaning they weren't punched in on the cash register, and she did not pay for them. Jeyja repeated the order to the customer. She showed the receipt and checked them together as she recounted the order.

"So you got two burgers, large fries, and five desserts. What else is missing?" Jeyja asked the customer.

"I am missing two burgers." The customer replied, looking confused.

"You didn't order it; we can punch your order so you can pay for it," Jeyja answered calmly.

Everything the customer ordered and paid for was in the bag and accurate.

"It's your fault. Just give me the four burgers, and it should be done!" the customer yelled at Jeyja.

'Huh? Four burgers? Didn't she say two burgers only?' I thought. I was listening to their conversation.

The customer blamed us for not hearing her order correctly. She wanted to get the food she didn't pay for since it was our fault that we didn't charge for everything she ordered.

The customer kept yelling at Jeyja, "I need the burgers! It's not my fault that you didn't hear me!"

Our manager, Antonio, intervened, resolved the situation, and apologized for the mistake. She removed her mask and raised her voice, "I don't have time for this!" My co-workers in the kitchen made her burgers quickly.

'Why do people need to make a scene? I understand we all make mistakes, but she's being extra.' I thought.

Jeyja went inside to where we did our delivery orders, and she cried. I hugged her and said, "The customer was an as*hole; don't mind her."

As I hugged her, Lolita said, "Hey, keep the distance."

We weren't supposed to hug or come near each other because we didn't know if one of us was carrying the virus, and we didn't want that to happen.

"Oops, sorry!" I was startled and moved away from Jeyja immediately.

I hate to see my co-workers being yelled at, especially if they are doing their jobs well. I hate to hear people yell at food workers or front-liners just because things didn't go well. I have been in a position where I did my job well, and people are still disappointed, still pointing out even our slightest mistakes.

Imagine doing your job so well and having a stranger yell at you. I didn't want others to experience that.

I understand that people were going through a rough patch during the pandemic, especially that year, but that should not be an excuse to be rude or feel superior to someone. Customers may have a right to complain, but they cannot degrade a worker making their food or whoever serves them.

I thought, *'We are fast-food workers and not your slave.'*

As fast-food workers, we tolerated so many hardships during the pandemic. We stayed still, comforted each other, and laughed at things we once took seriously.

13

A FRUSTRATED NURSE

I was wiping the front counter and trying to breathe while wearing a disposable mask and a face shield. We only had four more hours left before we closed the store. There were a few customers in the line. I washed my hands thoroughly since I needed to take orders. I was about to take orders when Antonio asked me to.

"Rainna, can you take the customer?" Antonio asked.

I was not fond of when I would do something, and the manager or someone at work would tell me what to do when I already knew what to do. I took the customer in line, carrying two tote bags and wearing a disposable mask and a face shield.

"Hi, can you call the supervisor who went that side?" the customer said, pointing to the online delivery area. She knew the supervisor for their uniform. I looked to the side she pointed to and saw *Mariano*. I approached *Mariano* and said, "Hey, the customer's looking for you." *Mariano* came up to the customer, and we didn't expect when the customer yelled at him.

She raised her voice, expressing her frustration with my supervisor for not wearing a mask. As a nurse, she emphasized the difficulties they encountered working every day, especially with the rising number of people falling sick and catching COVID-19 due to the lack of precautions.

"Why aren't you wearing a mask? You don't know how hard it is at the hospital! We are crowded and lack equipment!" the nurse lectured our supervisor.

I understood what the customer was trying to say and where she was coming from. It was already hard in the hospital, and she wanted us to protect ourselves and other people by wearing masks because if we didn't, we could catch the virus and might end up in the hospital.

The customer had a point, but she didn't know that our supervisor was on his break and waiting for his food. *Mariano* removed his mask because he needed to breathe for a while and threw a plastic bag into the office garbage bin. He then went to the online delivery area, where the nurse saw him.

I heard *Mariano* mumbling some words while the customer was still yelling at him, which was unnecessary.

"We are tired of all these people getting sick. I am a nurse, and you don't know what it is like to work in the hospital! You are the supervisor and should be the best example to your crew." She yelled with all her might towards our supervisor, *Mariano*.

'*She could have said it nicely.*' I thought.

I went to the hand washing station and washed my hands again, since I touched something sticky on the counter. *Mariano* wore a mask, took her order, and made her order right away.

Mariano could not move as he watched the customer go. He then walked to the kitchen and said, "I was on my break and wanted to drink some water."

"That was unnecessary; she could have said it nicely," I said.

"Just leave it, *Mariano*." My co-worker said.

"Yeah, exactly. She didn't have to yell." *Mariano* said.

"She's probably stressed out," I added.

"Yeah. But still. She was so rude." *Mariano* said.

"Everyone is going through something nowadays," I said, leaving for my break.

I went on my half an hour break. My face was hot, and I could hardly breathe while working and wearing a mask and face shield. I threw my old mask and sanitized my face shield using hand sanitizer. I wore a new mask and went to the front of the store to pay for a water bottle.

"I forgot my reusable water bottle again," I told Jeyja.

She cashed me out using Antonio's card for food payments. I went back to the break room and sat there for a while. I felt my body shaking, and I could hardly breathe, but it was manageable. I took three deep breaths and drank 750 mL of bottled water I bought.

14

FISH MARKET

"Rainna, take the next customer, and Jeyja, go on your break. Josiah, can you cover for *Mariano*? Oh, Rainna, the customer is waiting. Please take the next guest right away," Antonio said.

"Rainna, tell the customer to wear a mask," Antonio said. "Rainna, take the next customer, and Lester, help Rainna."

"Josiah, just keep making chicken. We're going to have a lineup," said Antonio. Antonio's voice couldn't shut up, and it hurt my ears—mine and all of us in the store.

Antonio brought a mega speaker, which he used to announce when we needed to change our gloves and wash our hands. It was easier for him to use it because hearing people with a mask on was hard.

One time, I dreamed about his voice and thought I woke up with Antonio's voice in my ears. I could hear his voice even in my dreams. His voice was too loud, and he was making unnecessary noise.

I was wiping the counter, and a customer came in. When I saw the customer looking at our menu board,

I thought, *'I need to wash my hands first.'*

I went to the hand washing area, and Antonio saw me.

"Rainna, take the customer," Antonio said.

I continued washing my hands, wiped my hands with paper tower, and closed the faucet with the paper towel I used.

'You don't have to tell me that; I know what I'm doing.' I thought.

One of my pet peeves is when someone asks me to do something that I was about to do or tells me what to do. I had worked at a fast-food restaurant for years and knew what to do. I had the initiative to work. Nobody needs to tell me anything about what to do.

I then took the customer's order who only wanted fries and some ketchup.

"Rainna, take your break, and Bill, cover Rain," Antonio said in a fast, high-pitched voice. "*Mariano*, how long is the chicken? After that, bread more chicken because we have a lot of orders."

"Rainna, when you return after the break, cover Lester for bagging."

"Lester, before you go on break, sweep the floor. We're going to have a lineup. Let's go! Let's go, guys! Make more burger patties. *Mariano*, please keep an eye on the chicken."

'Oh my gosh, his voice could not shut up.' I thought, and I got irritated.

"Antonio, when are you going on break?" I asked him.

I needed to ask him because his mouth needed to take a break. I could not hear customers' voices because of Antonio's voice in the kitchen.

"He thinks it's going to help run the store if he talks like that," I told Chase. "Like, his mouth needs to chill."

We laughed but didn't say anything. I felt safe with Chase and could mean anything without judgment.

When Antonio had a day off, one of my co-workers said," It's so quiet today."

"Right? It's like a fish market when Antonio is here." I added.

"I could hear his voice in my dreams!" said Jeyja.

"Girl, same!" I agreed with Jeyja.

15

APPRECIATIVE CUSTOMER

When we opened some of our dining tables for customers to dine inside the store, we put plexiglass on each seat and by the cash register. The plexiglass is a transparent, shatter-resistant material that became the go-to solution for our fast-food restaurant. It served as a barrier to reduce exposure from other people dining in. However, some of our tables were unavailable due to social distancing, and we had to make space for each table seat.

A man came to our store and said, "Hi, is my order ready?"

"Under what name, sir?" I asked the man.

He ignored me and asked Lester, who was bagging the order items since he had taken the man's order.

"Hi, is my order ready?"

"No sir, twenty more minutes. We just..."

The man stormed out and said, "Why are you guys taking so long for my order to make? I just got back here after twenty minutes, and now I have to wait for another twenty minutes? Holy sh*t!"

The man asked me, "Can we dine here?"

"Yes, sir, you can. Let me just check quickly to see if there are available seats." I then went to check the dine-in and saw some available seats. I returned to the cash register and asked the man, "How many of you are dining in?"

"Just me and my wife." He answered.

"Okay, yep! We have available seats." I assured the angry customer.

Then, I grabbed the clipboard from the online order station and asked the man to write his name, his wife's name, contact number and their address. The man wrote down their names and didn't ask why we had to do that. But it was for safety reasons that if we got in close contact with someone caught with COVID-19, we would contact them and let them know that we've had close contact with someone positive for COVID-19, and they needed to isolate.

I had just started my shift, and all that greeted me was chaos. The kitchen staff was busy, and Chase, who always works in the front store, was calling to make more gravy. Macy, who used to work in the front store with me, knew what it was like to work there, and she ensured that we weren't waiting for the food order for a long time. Macy was running back and forth. I took the customer's orders on autopilot. I couldn't handle any more negativity and complaints because it felt overwhelming.

While taking orders, I barely drank water and couldn't go to the washroom. I took the last customer before my break. I asked the other customer if he was okay with waiting twenty minutes for his order to be made, and he was. I asked my supervisor if I could go to the washroom quickly, and my supervisor gave me a go. I went to the crew washroom, and someone was inside. My co-worker was waiting for the washroom as well.

"My bladder is gonna burst in any minute!" I said to Jeyja.

"Just hold on!" Jeyja said jokingly.

I ran back to the storefront and prepared the customers's orders. I didn't want to wait any longer for the washroom when I could do my job while waiting for the person in the washroom to finish.

After a few hours, I finally drank water and used the washroom. The man who had been complaining about the wait time and dined in returned and was looking for his phone. My co-worker cleaned the tables right after the man left. I asked my supervisor if a crew member had found a phone.

I asked the man what phone he had to ensure we had the same phone in the office. "It's an iPhone 6s, white, with a crack on the screen, " he said.

The phone he described was the same phone we had in the office. When I gave it to him, I asked, "Is this your phone?".

"Yeah, that's mine!" He took his phone and I left.

The man talked to Rolland. A few minutes later, they were looking for me because the man wanted to speak with me. That man was starting to get under my skin. I wished he had left when he got his phone or hoped he never returned to the store. I didn't want to see him ever again. I wouldn't say I liked the way he spoke to me rudely because he made my day terrible.

I approached the customer, and the man said, "Thank you so much. You're doing an excellent job. What is your name?"

I didn't expect him to say that, and I felt light-hearted hearing an appreciative customer. "My name is Rainna," I said.

"Thank you, Rainna." He said, and he tapped my shoulder, which made me feel uncomfortable.

I held the conversation and asked where he came from and how long he had been in Canada. We all made small talk with a stranger, not to make the situation awkward, but deep inside me, I just wanted him to leave.

He seemed like an unforgettable person. He forgot his phone and would undoubtedly forget my name as soon as he stepped out of the store.

16

SLOW DAY

After hours of non-stop taking orders, Antonio sent me on break for ten minutes. I changed my washable mask to a new one. I always brought extra masks with me. I put the dirty washable mask in a small plastic bag and wore a new one.

When I returned from my ten-minute break, I saw a customer in a winter jacket come in. He looked old and sick. Antonio assigned me back to the new station while my co-worker, Bill, was assigned to take orders outside the store.

We split the line outside, one for placing orders and one for both phone pick-up and online delivery orders. We also had to let some people in, including those lined up to place orders. No matter how much we tried communicating with them, some people needed help following a simple rule. The big signs we put outside the store didn't seem helpful. We still had to explain to the customer that there were protocols we had to follow.

"A customer is waiting, Rainna," Antonio said.

Lester was assembling the food order said, "He's still wearing a winter jacket. Hahaha!".

I laughed with Lester. It was sunny, and the customer who came in was wearing a winter jacket. *'Isn't he feeling hot in that jacket?'* I thought.

"Hi there! Welcome to our store; how may I help you?" I greeted the customer who was wearing a winter jacket.

I wanted to ask him if he was sick because if he was, we could not serve him. He was wearing a mask with teary eyes.

'I'll know with his voice if he was sick.' I assumed.

"Can I get a combo burger with fries and a drink?" he said.

He appeared unwell, but his voice sounded clear and normal. Typically, when someone is sick, their voice sounds blocked and stuffy; they exhibit a hyponasal voice.

"Will that be all for today?" I asked him.

"Yeah, that'll be it. On credit, please." He replied.

I entered his total on the card transaction so he could pay through the card.

"It's going to be less than five minutes; you can wait there on the side," I said, pointing to the direction where he could wait.

Lester walked up to me, whispering, "He's not sick, right?"

"Nope, I don't think so," said I.

Then, it was quiet. I watched people outside through our window glass. I saw two white cars parked in front of our store. They brought dogs and chairs for a car meet-up. Most people would meet up at the parking lot during the pandemic in the summer because they were outside, didn't have to wear masks, and we could not invite people inside the house for precaution.

After fifteen minutes at the new station, a family group entered our store. I had to walk faster to the entrance and inform them that only one person could enter the store if they wanted to order. The man, who I assumed was the father, asked me, "Are you guys open for dine-in?"

I apologized and explained that the dine-in area was not open and that only one person could enter if they wanted to order as a family. Our store's protocols were changing from time to time. The family took a few minutes to think; one of their kids struggled to wear a mask because it was too big for her face.

The mother decided what to do and said, "Just get burgers for the kids and whatever you wanna get."

She then took their children outside the store and waited there. I felt terrible for them as they were probably frustrated that they couldn't dine anywhere and take their kids out for fun, as most playgrounds and play game establishments were closed. After taking their order, some teenagers came and ordered small food items. The line gets crowded quickly.

"It's good to have this station, and it's faster," I told Antonio.

"Yeah, of course. It's my idea," he replied proudly.

He then moved me to take online orders and calls for pick-ups since Macy was going for a half-hour break. I had to cover Macy while she was on her break. Macy was my co-worker and a classmate in college during the pandemic. Our moms were friends as well.

"For now, just help with the online orders and come back here later if we get busy and when Macy is back," Antonio said.

"Okay." I said.

I headed to the online orders station between the office room and the storefront counter. No one has called since Macy left for break, and no customer is on site. I loved quiet and slow days, but we couldn't just stand by the counter and not do anything. We had to clean up and stock up what we needed for the front store.

Some days, I like what I do. I loved working with my work best friends and at the fast-food restaurant during the pandemic because it made me forget how difficult it was to live in such an uncertain era.

Most days, I wanted to stay home and do what most people on social media do, such as reading, crocheting, cleaning, etc. Perhaps I would do affiliate links marketing online if I wasn't working at the fast-food restaurant, but I would get bored if I didn't socialize with others. I am introverted and love staying at home, but it was different when I found people at work with whom I could work well and have great conversations.

17

RAINY SUNDAY

Churches were closed during the pandemic. Some Church services were operated online.

My faith was declining. Though I used to be a "good Christian girl," I chose to live ungodly because I wanted to fit in in the world. It may sound wrong, but I was tired of feeling left by my friends since I didn't drink and go out to parties. I had never stepped foot in clubs. Sometimes, I prayed when needed, especially when the pandemic hit. I asked God earnestly to protect my family, friends, and myself from catching the virus. Indeed, God answered my prayers, but I didn't have a relationship with God like I used to. That I knew deep inside of me.

I had a morning shift on Sunday, and Antonio asked me to serve the customer.

"I'm waiting for my order. It was three buckets of chicken, burger, and fries," the customer said.

She wore black eyeglasses, a disposable mask, and she had some white hairs. She was wearing an orange tank top and white shorts. With her eyeglasses on, she looked older, but her voice sounded my age, like a teenager.

I saw two plastic bags with food items on the counter, and I thought it was her order. I gave those two plastic bags to her without checking what was inside the plastic. The customer was in a hurry, and she left right away when I handed her the two plastic bags. Jeyja asked me to take orders.

"Do I take orders from the new station?" I asked.

"No, take orders from here at the storefront. It's not busy," she said.

"Hi there, what can I get for you?" I said, calling the customer in the line.

The customer wore a neon green hat, fitted jacket, sports shorts, washable black mask, and headphones on his neck. He looked like a runner. He looked at the menu board and took a few minutes. While the customer was still thinking about his order, Jeyja asked me to bag the orders.

Antonio was fixing the carpet on the floor and the divider by the entrance door. He was also wiping the tables, which was the team member's job. It was only me and Jeyja at the storefront. No customer was in the line; only the customer looked like a runner. The phone rang, and Macy answered to take orders from the phone.

The customer, who looked like a runner, mumbled some words I couldn't understand since he was wearing a mask, and I asked him politely to repeat what he said.

"What does it come with a burger combo?" He asked loudly.

While bagging the orders, I told the customer, "It comes with fries and a drink."

"Okay, just give me a moment." He took his time to choose once again while itching his head.

"Take your time," I told him.

I asked Jeyja for whom the order I was bagging was since there weren't customers on-site, only the guy I was taking orders.

"Whose order is this?"

"It's for the lady earlier, wearing an orange tank top," Jeyja said.

"Oh shoot!" I shouted with wide eyes open. I could not move. I was standing there by the bagging area in total paralysis, realizing I had given the order wrong to the customer wearing an orange tank top.

"Oopsies! I made a mistake! I'm sorry. I gave the wrong order!" I apologized to Jeyja.

After several minutes of overthinking, the customer, who looked like a runner, finally decided what to order.

"I would like to get a burger, fries, and drinks. And do you guys have muffins?" He asked.

'Do we have muffins on the menu board?' I wanted to ask the customer if he hadn't looked at the giant menu board for several minutes.

"No, we don't have muffins," I replied, disgusted. "Do you like your burger with cheese?"

"No, and no sauce in the burger." He specified.

'You might as well get no patty and no bun.' I said in my head.

I was punching in his order while Jeyja made the order for another customer who went outside and returned to pick up their order. She also placed an order for the one wearing a tank top and had to put another batch for the customer's order that was given to the wrong person.

My heart beat faster because the customer I gave the wrong order to might come back and get mad at us. Jeyja and I immediately placed the customer's order, who looked like a runner, since it was only a burger combo, which we had available then.

"So, what are we going to do? What if the customer whom I gave the wrong order comes back?" I asked Jeyja.

"We can just remake her order; just print the receipt in case she returns," Jeyja said.

A few minutes later, many people entered to place their orders and bought a lot of food. Jeyja asked the customers in the line if they had placed an order separately; if not, one person should go outside. Only one person was allowed per order.

There were about ten people; all looked like Asian teenagers.

"Hi there, welcome to our store. How can I help you?" I called the first customer on the line.

"Hi, can I get uhmm, what's inside the burger?" He asked

"It has.."

"Oh, actually, I'm going to get the chicken with, hmm…" He then looked behind him and asked his friends,

"Yo, fam, what are you guys gon get?"

"I'm not sure yet, bruh."

Then he turned to me, looked at the menu board and said, "I'm gonna get the chicken, mashed potatoes and some drinks or some sh*t like that, hahaha."

"Not very funny," I thought.

I punched his orders in, and he asked, "Can we dine in?"

"No, sorry, only takeouts," I replied.

"Okay. That'll be it." Said he.

The people lined up were loud, asking each other what they would get and laughing loudly. My co-worker, Chase, helped me out by taking orders. Jeyja was taking orders on the phone and online order deliveries.

When they finished ordering, we ran out of chicken. Rolland said, "The chicken will take about ten more minutes. Are there any customers in the line, Rainna?"

"No. No customers in the line." I responded.

"All orders are ready; we just need to bag them," Jeyjah added.

Five hours later, the customer I gave the wrong order never returned, and we never heard anything from her. She probably took more food items than what she ordered.

Then, it poured outside, and the sky darkened. I loved it when it was raining because I knew we wouldn't be busy. The store became quiet.

Since it wasn't busy, I went to the staff washroom, but somebody was there.

'Why is it always someone in the washroom?' I thought.

I then drank water and checked my phone, and got a message from Bruno.

"Hey gorgeous." Said Bruno.

I went to the front, walked up to Chase, and said, "Oh my gosh, aaahhhh, Bruno messaged me and called me gorgeous. HAHAHA!"

"Girl. I'm happy for you! How's everything with him?" Said Chase.

"He doesn't reply often. Maybe he's busy, but he said we would get married in Cro…" I said excitedly, even though I knew Bruno didn't mean it.

"Girl, for real?"

I laughed out loud. " I don't think he's serious, though. But we'll see." I said, giggling.

I went to the break room again and replied to Bruno's message: "Hey, handsome, how have you been?"

Then, I could finally use the washroom. I brought my phone to the washroom to see if Bruno would reply.

Two minutes later, he hasn't replied yet. *'Maybe he'll reply later.'* I thought. I returned to the front and cleaned the trays while discussing life with Chase.

I had a chaotic day since I started giving the wrong food order to the customer. I didn't feel like working since it was raining, and I wanted to stay home and be covered by my blanket. But getting a text message from Bruno, the one I liked, eased my day.

18

DELIVERIES WERE NOT AVAILABLE

"Hi, I have been waiting for my online order for about fifty minutes now." said the customer on the phone.

"Hi, your order has already been made and is ready for delivery," I replied.

"Oh, okay, because I have been waiting for it for so long." The customer said.

"Oh, I'm sorry about that. Let me check the online delivery app; give me a second." I told the customer.

I grabbed the tablet we used for online delivery and discovered no delivery drivers were available in the area.

'What should I say? They must cancel their order, or they could get their food from here.' I thought.

I opened my mouth, but nothing came out. The customer was still on the phone. I didn't know how to explain to the customers that we didn't have delivery drivers available.

"Uhm, your order is ready, but we don't have any drivers. Do you want to cancel your order then?" I said it, finally! I expected that the customer would understand.

"I've waited so long for my order, and this is what you're gonna tell me?" Said the customer.

'It's out of my control.' I thought.

"I'm sorry about that." I apologized to the customer.

Then, the customer hung up the phone. I checked the tablet we use for online orders again and saw three customers cancelled their orders.

Another customer called with the same issue, and he complained, "What kind of service do you guys have? You guys should call us right away!"

I told Nelia about our online delivery dilemma. "We can't do anything about it. If they want, they can cancel their orders," said Nelia.

The store was quiet since it was raining in May. That was also why we were flooded with online orders: customers preferred that their orders be delivered to their doorsteps rather than come to our store while it was raining. Online shopping and deliveries were common during the pandemic since we weren't allowed outside unless we needed to go to work or grocery. If I had to stay home and work from home, I would also have ordered through online food delivery. But I worked at a fast food restaurant, and I could buy food and take it home after my shift. Also, online shopping became my habit during the pandemic since the malls were closed, and there was nowhere to go to unwind my mind.

A delivery driver came with a big bag for food orders and picked up two big online orders, which had been sitting there for two hours. I helped him put the orders in the bag and thanked him.

Another customer called. He asked if we could cancel his order since he had been waiting so long.

"Sir, I'm sorry. We cannot cancel the order from our side. You have to do it on your app." I said to the customer.

"Oh, what the f*ck? It's your fault that we're not getting the orders." He said in a defeaning voice. Then he cussed a lot of times. I wanted to hang up the phone, but I cut him off by saying, "If you want, you can speak to the manager."

"No need. I'm not gonna buy here anymore. Piece of sh*t." Then he hung up the phone.

I took it personally because he said, "It's YOUR fault."

'Don't cry, don't cry, don't cry.' I thought. I was trying to tell myself not to cry and hold my tears.

Five online delivery drivers were available a few hours later, but no customer had come. I was the only team member in the front, and Nelia was doing some supervisory work in the office. Some people in the kitchen were talking from a distance.

Then, Nelia asked me to throw away the food that had been cancelled. I felt bad for throwing out food, but the food had to be thrown away because it had lost its freshness and was no longer safe to eat, leaving it cold and unappetizing

I shouldn't take it personally when a customer cussed out, but it hurt me slightly. Although I wasn't busy that day at work, I was emotionally tired. I got bombarded by a lot of customer complaints. When riding the bus after my shift, I kept telling myself that I handled the customers well, that it wasn't my fault, and that I did a good job. When I got home, I burst into tears and wrote a lot in my journals. I penned positive words and affirmations for my benefit. I realized that no one else could provide the validation I could give myself.

19

HEART BROKEN

In June 2020, the lockdown eased a bit, and people could finally visit other restaurants that opened late and closed early. However, there were still restrictions, and they had to wear masks upon entering the location. Some restaurants that were not fast food had long lineups and needed to book a table in advance.

Bruno and I planned to meet. I asked for his confirmation if we could still meet on the day we were supposed to meet.

Bruno replied, "Listen, I can't love you; I can't be in a relationship or anything like one. I also can't just use you for sex. Not that type of guy. I'd feel like sh*t after."

I didn't open his message for a while, but I could read his message through my phone's notification. My heart shuttered in pieces upon seeing his message for me.

'*Oh, I thought we were something. I thought we were about to enter into a relationship. Was I being delusional? Why did I believe in your flirtatious lips?*' I said to myself.

I read his message repeatedly until I opened it and replied, "Okay, I understand that. Thanks for telling me."

I respected him for being brutally honest, and I was grateful for that, but the pain in my heart was intense and overwhelming, hitting me in waves. It was the kind of grief that was both physical and emotional, leaving me feeling drained and unable to focus on even the simplest of tasks.

I started questioning myself again whether I was enough for somebody to love me.

'Why do I always get heartbreak from someone I love?' I thought. *'I hope that this pain's edges will dull with time.'*

My heart is a sharp shard of glass that has lodged itself deep within my gut, causing a constant ache that never seems to fade. I then realized that I had fallen in love with Bruno and everything that fell broke.

I checked the COVID-19 case status to see how many cases there were in Canada. I watched movies to distract myself, but when Bruno's voice echoed in my ears as I watched movies and drama series, my heart was slowly tearing down again.

A wave of sadness swept over me as I covered myself in a blanket at 19 degrees Celsius outside. I opened his message and reread it; it felt like a part of me had been ripped away. While looking at my room's ceiling, in moments of stillness, I felt like it could take over my entire being. The grief that comes with heartbreak was gruelling, stealing my appetite and sleep and leaving me feeling numb and lost.

I went outside my room to find my cat and brought her with me for entertainment. Then, I covered myself in a blanket again. Since my cat didn't want to stay in my room, I would give her treats. I needed emotional support, but I didn't know whom to call or text to explain my situation with Bruno.

Then I remember Chase.

'When I return to work, I will tell Chase everything.' I thought.

I couldn't see Bruno for a long time. I told him in March that I would like to see him after the lockdown, then he said, "It's gonna be a long wait." The lockdown kept on extending. I was upset that I didn't get a chance to see Bruno before the lockdown. I wish I had seen him before the pandemic hit. I wished I hugged him tighter. I missed his voice and his face when he smiled and squinted his eyes. I missed the way he made me feel alive during the conversation. But at the same time, I was struggling with my insecurity. I was not confident in myself because I didn't have much experience in life like Bruno. I was lightweight and couldn't drink much like he could. I wish I could hold his hands like we did while walking by the lake, kiss him one more time, and hear his deep, loving voice again, but it was too late. The pandemic created a physical and emotional distance between me and Bruno, leading to hardships and challenges that impacted us, or perhaps we weren't meant to be.

Part

II

THE PEOPLE INSIDE THE FAST FOOD

20

THE GOOD SUPERVISORS

Nelia was by far one of my favourite supervisors. She was quiet but greeted the team members when they came in and helped us with big orders.

One morning, I had big orders through online delivery, and of all the people in the kitchen and front, only Nelia helped me out. She ran back and forth to get food items to make it easier for me. She asked for food items in advance to make them ready and speed up the service.

"Thank you very much!" I told Nelia.

"You're welcome, Rain. Just let me know if you need help," she said.

When she helped me, it lit up my heart, and I knew then that she was kind-hearted. When we got quiet at the store, and there was no customer in sight, Chase and I talked about Bruno at the front counter while pretending we were busy.

Then, I realized two online delivery orders were pending, and I didn't hear the beeping sound. Nelia said, "We need fifteen chicken pieces for delivery orders and five burgers."

When I heard the "delivery order," my heart dropped in fear, and I ran to the online delivery area.

"That's okay, Rain. I'll do it. It's just two orders." Nelia said.

I felt bad for neglecting my responsibility for online delivery orders. I helped Chase to assemble the order. I only have a few memories of Nelia because she took months off from work.

When she returned, as soon as I walked into my workplace, Nelia greeted me with such enthusiasm that it was like a breath of fresh air.

She excitedly greeted me, "Hi Rain, how have you been? It's been a long time since we last saw each other."

Her warmth and kindness made my heart light up, but at the same time, I felt like Nelia deserved better than working at a fast-food restaurant. Although I wanted to talk to her more and get to know her closely, we didn't have the opportunity since we always got busy, and I needed to be more open when initiating conversations with her.

Despite her helpful attitude, I heard Nelia often got into trouble at work. Our manager, Antonio, usually told her to let the team members do their jobs, but Nelia continued assisting us anyway. It was clear that she genuinely cared about the well-being of her colleagues and was always willing to lend a helping hand.

The supervisors weren't supposed to do what the team members should do because the supervisors needed to watch the people coming in, and they had to keep an eye on the food products and the team members.

❦❦❦

I started working the same month Nessa joined Fast Food. Nessa had only been to Canada for three months when she joined the fast-food restaurant where I work. We barely got a chance to talk because of the chaos at fast food.

One time, Nessa and I both caught our eyes, looked at each other and smiled. She was in the kitchen, and I was at the front. Lolita went to the kitchen and taught Nessa something.

Nessa was hired as a supervisor; it could have been my position if I had taken the offer, but I was glad I declined it. They trained Nessa everywhere because a supervisor needed to learn everything at the store, and they had to learn quickly.

One of my afternoon shifts, Nessa was the supervisor at the front. While the restaurant got busy, Antonio and Lolita were in the kitchen and watched Nessa. Nessa helped us take orders and bagged the food items.

"Nessa, leave the job to the team members. You're not supposed to do it. Just observe and instruct the team members," Antonio said in a high-pitched voice.

"What are you doing? You're not helping; you are making the service worse." Lolita said to Nessa.

I felt terrible for Nessa and deeply embarrassed for Lolita and Antonio for yelling at a worker in front of many customers.

'Why can't they talk to her in the office?' I thought.

I stopped taking orders since many customers were in the front, waiting for their orders. I understood why Antonio and Lolita needed Nessa to step out of the picture to see what needed to be done. If Nessa continued working with the team members, she wouldn't be able to check the service because she was busy doing the team members' jobs.

I couldn't understand that the management team, except for Nessa and Nelia, had a habit of shaming the workers in front of other people. What would they feel if it happened to them what they were doing to other workers?

It was another busy day. Nessa was again assigned as the front store supervisor. In the kitchen, Adrianna said, "Nessa, don't help the team members. Just watch the line." We had restrictions on letting people in the store, and someone, especially a supervisor, needed to watch out for people coming into the restaurant. Adrianna was one of my favourite supervisors, and her presence in the workplace was always a source of joy. She could lighten the mood, often joking around and sharing laughs with us team members, which created a friendly and supportive atmosphere. I truly admired her because she excelled at her responsibilities and inspired me to do my job well. For Adrianna, being a supervisor was more than a job; it was a genuine passion she pursued wholeheartedly.

"Nessa, why do we have so many people? Why do we have so many people in the line?" Antonio said to Nessa.

Nessa went to the entrance doors and told the last few customers to wait outside because the store was "too crowded" for having ten customers in the line. I then started bagging the orders that Nessa had left on the counter.

Nessa and I worked the closing shift. We finally got a chance to talk about our lives. She said she had been to Canada for three months, was married, and was five years older than me.

I felt bad again for her because she shouldn't have experienced a brutal way of working while adjusting to a new country. I could see in her eyes that she was tired, and I could feel she didn't want to work at the fast-food just like I did. I appreciated Nessa for helping us, and I could feel that she was nervous at that moment.

I remember seeing her at the counter. I walked up to her and asked, "Hey Nessa, are you okay?" She didn't respond, and she continued wiping the counter. I thought she was going to burst into tears.

When Lolita quit, I saw Nessa in the dining room. I approached her and said, "Hey, Lolita is gone!"

"Oh my gosh! Yes, finally! She's gone! I thanked God that she had left already!" she said happily.

I could see joy in her eyes. She told me all the hurt she'd gotten from Lolita, and every time Lolita talked to her, it made her fear coming to work. She felt like she was in a cage, and higher management constantly watched her moves. Nessa was approachable and kind, and I hated how the management treated her. She continued doing her job as a good supervisor.

※※※

We opened a new store around Toronto, but it was a trailer-truck type of store. It had tight spaces and was hot, and Ralph had to work 14 hours from opening to closing the truck store. They had installed the truck store as a test to see if it would be effective in selling. I had never been there or seen what the truck looked like.

Ralph was one of the nicest supervisors, and he was the reason I got the job. His brother, Scott, was a friend of mine. They are goodhearted and kind people.

The management team had a meeting one afternoon at work, but one supervisor needed to be present at the store. Ralph was the present supervisor. Two people called in sick, one at the kitchen and one at the front.

When things got hectic, Ralph attempted to handle multiple tasks simultaneously. He simultaneously prepared two batches of fries and instructed the kitchen staff to increase the production of burger patties and soup to accommodate the busy period.

The floor in the kitchen had chicken crumbs, and the sink was full of dishes. The line outside was until the exit door. It was about ten yards long from the entrance.

Ralph helped me assemble the orders, but he had to run back and forth from the kitchen to the storefront. Some customers asked us how long their orders would take to complete since they had been waiting a long time.

Some plastic bags and cups were on the hazardous floor. We ran out of chicken and had to stop taking orders for a while. I wiped the counter while one of my coworkers swept the floors. It was getting darker, and many people were still coming in.

My heart sank seeing Ralph going from place to place. He had exerted himself to the fullest, as evidenced by the weariness and exhaustion etched on his eyes.

'He deserved a better and good-paying job.' I thought.

He is calm like Nelia, but Ralph is a gangster for being fearless and uncompromising. He quit within 24 hours of notice, "It's my last day." he never returned to fast food. He couldn't work more at the trailer truck for fourteen hours.

"I aspire to be like Ralph one day. Hahaha." I said to Chris.

"I know, right? Same, same." Said Chris.

⚘⚘⚘

As someone who has worked at a fast-food chain since my teenage years, I don't recommend adults with children to work at a fast-food type of job. Not only does it pay a minimum wage, but it is also challenging to find someone to cover a shift, especially if it is a last-minute call in sick. Fast-food chain jobs can be a great way to earn money, but they shouldn't be the only source of income.

I felt terrible on Norman's first day at fast food because I could see how Antonio talked to Norman badly. As a new supervisor, Norman was still trying to learn things like other workers who just started a new job. Norman was trying to familiarize the menu, how we work, and how to deal with complaints.

I heard Antonio telling Norman how to do things in an angry tone of voice. *'You could have said that nicely.'* I thought.

One day, Norman didn't come to work. It was a huge issue when a supervisor didn't come to work because the present and on-duty supervisors had to carry an extra workload. I didn't know why Norman didn't show up for his shift until one day when Antonio was not on shift, and Norman and I had a gossip session in the kitchen; Norman told me what had happened.

Norman had an emergency. His daughter was sent to the hospital, and he said to Antonio, "Hi Antonio, I won't be able to come tomorrow since I have an emergency."

"Is there any way you could make things work to come in tomorrow?" Said Antonio.

My eyes widened when I heard Antonio request that of Norman, and I was stunned to speak.

"Wait, what? For real?" I said in a shock.

"Yeah." Norman said.

"Well, obviously, your priority is your daughter. He has kids, too. He should understand." I said angrily.

I didn't know much about Norman, but I'm sure he didn't deserve to be treated like that. I didn't know why Antonio would say such a thing. Other than that, Norman was a good supervisor. He helped as much as possible and was not just a supervisor but a friend to us as workers. He humbled himself as a human being and as a worker.

21

LOLITA

"Rolland, can I have a change for one-hundred-dollar bill?" I asked Rolland.

"No, you can't," he said jokingly and laughed.

"Please? If you give me a change, then you are handsome. Haha!" I said.

"I'm always handsome." He replied.

We both went to the office, and our supervisors cleaned and threw away old employees' files. Lolita, one of the supervisors and my co-worker Danica went to the office for an incident report.

Rolland opened the vault where they kept money and said, "Don't look." I laughed and said, "As if I'm interested in knowing the vault password." Still, I was more interested in Lolita and Danica's conversation in the office. Lolita was mad at Danica for calling in sick. I saw Danica was about to cry.

We have a stringent policy when an employee calls in sick. If someone is to call in sick at work, they have to find someone who would replace them for the shift, which we didn't like about the management. We didn't have everyone's phone number. We thought it should have been the supervisor's job. Upon working at my previous job as a Team Leader at the coffee shop, I would find someone to replace the employee who would be absent for the shift.

"Please don't talk to me like that," Danica said with teary eyes. Her voice cracked a little bit.

"I always tell you if you call in sick, make sure you find someone to cover you. We were short yesterday, and it was the weekend. How many times do we have to tell you? You've been working for so long, and this is not the only time you've done such a thing. Here, you have to sign and write what you did." said Lolita angrily, handing Danica the disciplinary action form.

Danica was staring blankly at Lolita.

I was scared Lolita would yell at me. Danica took the paper to the breakroom, wrote down what she had done, and signed it.

Rolland gave me a change and asked him to open the tills for me. Only the management team could open the cash registers, and we had to ask them first if we needed to take or put something in the till.

"What else do you need from me?" Rolland asked sarcastically.

"Your whole being. Haha!" I said jokingly. "Can you work for me, too?" I said weirdly, joking.

"Wow! No thanks!" he said, and he went to the kitchen.

"I'm quitting," said Danica.

She went to the office to give the form to Lolita. Lolita and Danica were in the office. Lolita slammed the office door. I heard them talking distinctly. I knew from that moment that Danica would quit.

Danica and I were not that close, but we mainly talked at work. When we had downtime, we talked about our lives and what we wanted in the future. A few months later, Danica quit Fast-Food job because she was going back to school and because of Lolita and the toxic environment in our workplace.

In February 2020, before the lockdown, Lolita said, "Rainna, don't talk too much to the customers; make them faster.".

It was a busy afternoon, and I talked to the customer about what cashiers would do. I asked the customer how his day had been, and it was small talk. I had a small talk with about ten customers in a row, and Lolita noticed that the line was not moving because I took time to take their orders and talked too much with the customers.

Then, on an afternoon shift, Lolita was also working, and she fought with *Mariano* because he was being slow in the kitchen.

They had been fighting like cats and dogs. I didn't mind them arguing, I just did my job because I wasn't planning in staying at fast food. While Lolita and *Mariano* were arguing, I did the same thing I used to; I would talk to the customer and ask how their day had been. I liked talking to the customers, especially when I saw them smile, and it made me feel excited about socializing. Then, Lolita approached me from the kitchen and said, "You need to work faster, Rainna; this is a fast-food restaurant. It is okay to talk with the customer, but make it faster." She said this right before me in the presence of many customers.

'*This is a fast-food restaurant, so is customer service.*' I said to myself.

I took the next customer's order and didn't ask how their day had been. I just took the customer's order, took their payments, and said, "Thank you."

It was boring, but I got used to it later on. Lolita might have been a supervisor for a long time, but she needed to learn how to correct an employee properly. Management should not verbally discipline an employee in front of the people; instead, it should be done privately.

Lolita fought with many customers when adopting the "new normal" system during the Pandemic. She fought with a customer who had the same attitude as her.

One day, while the customers were waiting for their order, she asked the married couple, "Can you social distance with each other?"

The customer said, "No. This is my husband. We live together. Why do we need to social distance?"

"This is the new protocol; just follow it. You are inside our store, and you should follow what I say, " Lolita told the married couple.

"Wow! You're telling me these things as if you own this place. Who are you to say that?" Said the customer.

"I am a supervisor here, and we are following the rules and protocol because we want to ensure everyone's safety!" Lolita said.

"We don't need social distancing because it doesn't make sense. We live at home and sleep together in one bed," said the customer.

Lolita walked to the office while the customer was still talking to her. "I just wanted to ensure my workers are safe. That's all I care about." Lolita said to Antonio.

"Even so, you should ask the customers to social distance nicely." I overheard them in the office while I was washing my hands.

"Are you okay?" *Mariano* asked me.

"Yeah, I am. Can I go on my break now?" I asked *Mariano*. Whenever *Mariano* came up to me and talked, it made me feel uncomfortable.

"Yeah, you can. Go for a 15-minute break."

"Thanks," I said. We only had a ten-minute paid break, but *Mariano* gave me 15-minute breaks.

"Can you punch my order? I'm just gonna get a burger with cheese." I said to *Mariano*.

While I was talking to *Mariano*, the customer Lolita fought with walked up to me and asked for Lolita. The office door was closed because Lolita and Antonio were talking privately, so I left the issues with *Mariano* because I was also about to take my break.

"The customer asked for Lolita. Can you call her?" I said to *Mariano*.

"Yeah, don't worry about it." He said to me, punched in my food for my break on the cash register, and talked to the customer.

I went to the break room and ate. I was grateful for not taking the supervisory position, especially since it was more challenging to be a supervisor during the Pandemic because everybody was adjusting to the protocols—not only the customers but even us workers.

As a fast-food worker working at the cash register area, it was hard for me to deal with customers; telling them to wear a mask and reminding them about social distancing was hard enough for me. I could not imagine being a supervisor, dealing with difficult people, managing the sales, implementing the new protocols and juggling other stuff for supervisory duty.

⚘⚘⚘

In 2022, Chris told me stories about Lolita. He used to be a cashier before he started working in the kitchen. Chris had always been one of my closest friends at work, someone I could rely on for support and camaraderie. It wasn't until he returned to Fast Food after he left due to some reasons that I discovered we shared several mutual friends. This revelation sparked countless conversations in the break room, where we often caught up and exchanged stories. The atmosphere was filled with laughter and lively gossip as we chatted over our break time. We almost forgot about the pandemic since we talked much about our lives and the people we knew before the pandemic hit.

One day, Lolita was assigned to be the supervisor at the storefront. She was tasked with managing the staff for their breaks, helping them out, and dealing with customer complaints.

Lolita assigned Chris to the bagging area. He had to pack the orders and give the bagged food items to the customers.

Chris reminisced, "I was a new employee working at a fast-food restaurant for about a month back then. Lolita was the supervisor." Chris said to me.

Then he continued his story. "I forgot to check the customer's receipt before giving their order, and Lolita yelled at me because of that. It was busy, and many customers were waiting for their orders in the front. That mother f*cking Lolita yelled at me just because I made a mistake for not checking the customer's receipt."

"Dang, and what did Lolita say?" I asked him.

"She said, 'You're supposed to check the receipt first before giving the orders; Blah Blah Blah, what if you gave them the wrong orders? You cannot make mistakes. What if the customer got mad?' Like what the f*ck? Then she invaded my personal space." Chris shared, feeling pissed about what happened back then.

"How?" I wondered how Lolita invaded Chris's personal space because that was bizarre.

"She would follow me everywhere! She went to the store just to tell me my mistakes!" he said.

"Eww! I mean, Wow! As if she never made mistakes in her life. I understand they were trying to avoid customer complaints, but they shouldn't act as if you made a huge mistake." I told Chris.

"Yeah, yow, and it was traumatizing," Chris said.

"But did you give the order to the right customer without checking their receipts?" I asked.

"Yeah, because there were no customer complaints at that time." He said.

Chris told me stories about the former employees as well. There's this girl named Holly and the other worker, who he could not remember the name of; they were laughing at the storefront while it was downtime. No customers were in sight and were already stocked up, so they were talking like other workers would. Lolita heard them laughing. She called them into the office and had written up a disciplinary action form for laughing.

"I can't believe Lolita. She was just unbelievable." Said I.

Lolita was indeed unbelievable. While I was still working with her, I kept a civil and straightforward conversation with her. I would do whatever she asked me to do to avoid her getting mad at me. I remember her telling me that she also worked at a coffee shop in another province, and I told her that I worked at a coffee shop as well. We had shared our experiences with coffee shop jobs. Since then, she has been friendly and spoke to me nicely.

Perhaps I was lucky enough to only work with her for a few months because I didn't want to experience what my co-workers had experienced dealing with her for the longest time. Or maybe all these times, she was being misunderstood. Perhaps she had a kind heart, but she wanted to act tough so that people wouldn't disrespect her. I didn't know much about Lolita, but I am sure she was not "pure evil," as my co-workers would call her.

22

RELIGIOUS MARTIN

"Can I buy you, Rainna? How much are you?" Martin said while standing beside the counter.

He placed his mask below his chin while holding a cup of water. I looked at him and fakingly laughed. His words embarrassed me since he was three decades older than me.

I was taking my co-worker's order since she wanted some food to take home for her dinner. We were about to close then, and her shift had ended. She threw her mask into the trash can and ordered some food. Most of my co-workers would remove their masks when their shift ended, but I wore mine every time except when I was home.

Then, as I was preparing my co-worker's order, Martin walked up to me and said, "How are you, Beautiful?"

I said, "I'm doing good; we're almost done, eh?"

Then he said, "Yeah, I'm quitting."

"For real, though?" I asked surprisingly. Deep inside my head, I thought, *'Yes, finally, you're quitting.'*

He answered, "Yeah, because I was hired as a stockman but they asked me to wash dishes. I didn't apply for that."

"Oh, so true. And you get what? A minimum wage for doing a lot of work," said I.

"Yeah, it's unfair, so I'm quitting," said Martin.

"Oh, that's okay. You still have another job," said I.

Then he said, "Yeah, anyway, just bring the dishes to the sink when you finish. Okay, beautiful?"

"Okay," I said, not looking at him.

My eyes widened, and my heart beat faster. *'It can't be another Mariano,'* I said in my head. *'Why would a man three decades older than me ask me if he could buy me? I am not an object! If he was joking, then it was not a good joke.'*

I gave my coworker's order. "Thank you, and take care!" I said, and we said goodbyes. She left, and I brought the dirty dishes to Martin.

"Thank you, beautiful," Martin said.

My thoughts tumbled over each other, a jumbled mess of 'what-ifs': *'What if Martin is another Mariano?'* My heart pounded as if it was keeping up with my anxiety. I had a gut feeling that there was something wrong with Martin. I wouldn't say I liked how he talked, and it was bizarre that he asked me if he could buy me and call me beautiful.

"You're flirtatious, Martin. You flirt with the pretty people at the store." Andrew said in the kitchen.

I walked back to the front and heard Martin say, "Why? She's beautiful. Right, Rainna?" I pretended that I didn't hear it and continued walking to the front, where I started cleaning the counter and wiping off the trays.

I never liked Martin as a worker. I wanted to respect him because he was older; we should respect our elders in Filipino culture. Besides,

Martin was a religious person. He would play some worship song in the back of the store sometimes, but if he were another *Mariano*, the former supervisor who gave me trauma, I could not respect Martin, and I would have said something to get him to shut up.

☟☟☟

I heard interesting stories from Chris about our co-workers and Martin. When we had downtime at work, we would talk about our co-workers. Sometimes, we would hang out at home with Chris's loving girlfriend, Jena, and discuss things we could not discuss at work.

One time, when Chris and another co-worker were in the break room, Martin saw a Facebook post of Clara, one of our co-workers. Martin said, "Clara has big boobs and butt, ouhhh she's got big boobs and butts. ouhhh yeah." They were silent in the breakroom while Martin was talking about Clara. Chris could not believe that Martin would say that. Martin could not be joking either because even if he was a joker, he could not joke about women if he was sensible.

Then, one time, Martin showed Jane, our co-worker as well, a sexy picture of a woman in a bikini and said while showing the picture, "This girl is so hot, but it would be hotter if you're in this bikini."

I was stunned to speak, and I could not fathom my thoughts. Clara and Jane were not in their 20s yet; they were still young, and the "religious" Martin would say those things.

"Is he trippin'?" I asked Chris.

"No, he's serious, though, and he bragged about his daughter taking a religious program in Australia."

"What the f*ck?! And he's a devoted Christian, too." I said in amazement. I was still processing my thoughts. "Well, I'm glad he quit."

"Yeah, man. He quit because there were a lot of dishes to be washed, and he had a lot of things to do," said Chris.

"Yeah, that makes sense," I said.

It was perplexing that he claimed to be a devout Christian while having fantasies about the women at work. I'm also a Christian and not perfect, so I can't judge him. I claimed to be a Christian, yet I would cussed out. But even if he was not a devoted Christian, it was still inappropriate for him or anyone to fantasize and engage in sexual conversations around younger people.

23

MARIANO

Although I was deeply in love with Bruno, rumours quickly spread that *Mariano* and I were having an affair at work.

On my first day at work in January 2020, I arrived five minutes before my shift started at five o'clock in the afternoon. One of our supervisors, *Mariano*, approached me and introduced himself. It was funny how most supervisors didn't know it would be my first day as if I had come by surprise.

They assigned me to the kitchen, specifically at the gravy station, where we pour gravy into containers. There were two gravy stations: the one where we cooked the gravy and the one where we poured the gravy into containers for customers.

Mariano was assigned as supervisor for the kitchen area. His primary duty was to ensure that the fried chicken, soups, and burger-making patties were prepared and cooked to the highest standards. He monitors the production process, constantly assessing the demand and instructing the kitchen staff when to make more patties and chicken to meet the requirements of the restaurant.

I stood beside *Mariano*, and he showed me how to pour the gravy into the containers. When it was my turn, he asked about my age, how long I had been in Canada, and if I was attending school. It was a typical conversation for me, especially since it was my first time meeting the person.

"How old are you?" I asked *Mariano*.

He hesitated to answer my question, and then one of the kitchen workers asked *Mariano* if they needed to make more patty. *Mariano* paused as he removed a tray from the hot shelves. Perhaps he didn't know whether to answer me or the other worker first.

Then, *Mariano* answered me first, saying, "I'm 32."

He turned to the other worker and said, "Yeah, make more patties; we have a lineup."

I asked *Mariano* the same thing he asked me. I felt embarrassed for asking him and felt everyone was listening to our conversation.

Then, *Mariano* asked, "Do you have a boyfriend?"

I noticed he was trying to get to know me and wanted to learn about my personal life, but I brushed it off. I didn't want to think anything wrong since I just started working. *Mariano* was ten years older than me. I initially thought he was friendly, so I didn't mind him asking me if I was single.

"Yeah, I am single," I said.

I didn't ask him if he was single, but he said, "I've been out of a relationship for five years since my ex fooled me."

"Oh, sorry about that. Five years down the drain, eh?" I said.

"Yeah, it sucks, but it is what it is," he answered.

He kept looking at me, but I didn't bother asking why. Maybe it was because I was new and he was unfamiliar with my face, or perhaps he had seen someone like me. We were talking just like ordinary co-workers, and then he sent me for my break and said, "You would get half an hour's unpaid break and a ten minutes paid break."

Throughout my shift, I poured gravy and filled out some forms. By the end of my shift at midnight, *Mariano* gave me my worker's ID number and a code for punching our break. He asked me to put my phone number on a piece of tissue paper. I thought it might be needed for work, so I wrote down my phone number. I noticed a slight smile on his lips.

"Is it okay if I leave now? I have to catch the last bus," I asked *Mariano*.

"Yeah, go ahead! Take care!" *Mariano* said, looking at me intensely.

As I got off the bus and walked down my street, *Mariano* texted me that night. At first, I didn't mind him texting me late at night since he was a co-worker.

"Hey, it's *Mariano*. It's nice meeting you. Did you get home safe?" he said in his text message.

"Yeah, I am. Thanks for training me today!" I replied. He replied quickly, but I didn't reply as I felt something was wrong when he said, *'Did you get home safe?'*

While showering that night, I couldn't stop thinking and questioning that one line. *'Why did he have to make sure I was safe? Oh, perhaps he just cared that the new employee got home safe because if not, I guess they would have to find someone to replace me, right? I guess?'* I convinced myself.

I had the same shift the next day. In a text message, I asked *Mariano*, "How would I know when I work next? The manager, Antonio, just told me to come in today at the same time, five o'clock."

Then *Mariano* replied within 30 seconds of my message, "Good morning. Did you sleep well? I will show you later where we put the schedule."

"Okay, thanks! Aren't they supposed to send us through email?" I asked.

Again, he replied fast and said, "No. There is a binder where we put the schedule."

I didn't reply. Then he double-texted me and said, "How are you going to the store?"

"I'm gonna take the bus," I said.

We exchanged messages, and I felt awkward. My instinct told me that something was wrong with our conversation.

'This supervisor is tryna get close to me.' I thought.

Perhaps the gossip had started when some of our co-workers had seen us together going home. I asked *Mariano* to ride me home twice in February. I needed a ride home because I couldn't download the Uber app from my phone since my phone's memory capacity was full back then. I didn't know that asking a supervisor for a ride was wrong, but our store closed at midnight every day before the pandemic lockdown. Since *Mariano* was at least a close co-worker, it was 2:00 after midnight, and no bus was available; I asked him if he could give me a ride home. Also, when I finally downloaded the Uber app on my phone, the second time I asked him for a ride was because Uber had declined my credit card. I didn't pay my minimum payment for my credit card, so I had to wait for my next paycheck. I tried calling the cab, but the other line kept hanging up. They might have some technical problem with their line.

Days went by, and we were in February 2020. The news about COVID-19, Kobe Bryant's death, wildfires in Australia, and a possible WW3 were still topics on social media, and many memes were made about the news. That was what some people would do: make a joke out of everything on the news to make fun of. But I was not complaining. Some meme jokes were funny and relatable; I would share them on my Instagram story or send them to my friends through group chat messages on WhatsApp.

Whenever I post on my Instagram story, I check who views my Instagram story. I always waited for Bruno to view it, which would mean a lot to me. My mindset was set as if Bruno viewed my story, which meant he still wanted to talk to and meet me. I was young, naive, and in love with Bruno. I wouldn't say I liked it when I was expecting a text from Bruno, but I got *Mariano's* message instead. I wish every text notification I get were from Bruno, and it broke my heart when a text came, and it wasn't from him.

Mariano texted me every hour. I didn't reply to his messages because I only saw him as a friend and felt uncomfortable with how he communicated with me through texting. When I had a snowboarding accident before the pandemic lockdown, I had to let the managers know I wouldn't be working for a week, including *Mariano*.

"They said if I feel weird in few days, then I'll have to go get it checked." I said to Mariano.

"I think it's better to get checked I wanna make sure you are fine so that I don't have to worry," said he. "So you can't even get out of bed?"

I didn't reply to his messages because I wanted to rest and not talk to *Mariano*.

"How's your head though?" He messaged me again.

"You don't have to worry," I said.

I had felt a little bit of freedom from *Mariano* when my family doctors asked me to stay away from texting and working since my head needed recovery from a mild concussion due to a snowboarding accident.

Mariano messaged me a lot, making it evident that he wanted attention to the point that it got on my nerves.

I said, "Don't text me again unless it's about work."

He said, "Yeah okay. I will not text you again, sorry.

"Thanks," said I.

Then he kept messaging me, saying,

> "No problem"
> "Just keep in touch when you can"
> "If you ever need anything, I'm here, okay?"

'Oh my goodness! When are you going to stop?' I thought.

I told *Mariano* to keep things professional because of how he looked at me, and his messages made me uncomfortable. Still, he kept messaging me for a few weeks even though I didn't reply to his messages. I told him twice not to send me messages if they were not work-related. I only asked him about my work schedule since I didn't want to call the store or have anybody's phone number.

'I wish I didn't ask him for a ride,' I thought.

24

PCR AND ISOLATED

I woke up for my morning shift fatigued and with a runny nose. My throat and lips were dry.

'Did I catch the virus?' I asked myself.

I brushed my teeth and took a shower quickly. I skipped breakfast most of the time since I didn't have enough time to eat, and I would sleep in every day for work. I didn't feel like bussing, so I called for Uber since I wasn't feeling well. I sneezed a lot and had a runny nose.

One of the symptoms of COVID-19 was a runny nose. I had COVID-19 symptoms in the last week of May. It was spring, and the sun was out, but we still had to wear lightweight jackets and masks inside and outside the establishment. The bus policy had changed, and about 15 people were taken inside with precaution, one person per 2–3 seats at a time on the bus.

When I got to work, I heard gossip that one of our co-workers had caught COVID-19. I worked with her at online delivery. We bumped into each other as we worked in a small place for online delivery. I worked with that person for hours, and we talked without staying six feet apart. My heart beat faster, and my hands were sweaty when I heard the gossip.

'What if I got close contact with that person while they're carrying the virus?' I thought.

I had to remain calm while working, but I could not stop overthinking that I might have caught the virus. Antonio had put me to work on online delivery orders. I had to punch in every order we received at the cash register and prepare for online food orders.

"Macy, we're gonna need more soups for delivery order," I said with a hyponasal voice.

"Okay, got it!" Macy said.

A few hours later, it got busy before I went for my break. Many customers started lining up, and I had to stop punching online orders on the cash register since I had to bag the ready online deliveries. Macy helped me to bag the orders for online deliveries. I had forgotten about my sickness as my mind and body were occupied with work and what needed to be done.

"Do you guys need help?" Jeyja asked.

I answered, "Yes, please!"

"What else do you guys need?" Jeyja asked.

"We need more burgers, fries, and soups," said I.

The delivery driver, wearing a mask and face shield, asked me, "How long has this order been?" and showed me the phone with the customer's name.

I said, "It's not ready yet."

I then checked the online delivery tablet and had twelve orders.

"Oh my gosh, there's a lot of orders!" I exclaimed.

"Macy, go back to the kitchen; they need help there," Antonio said.

BEHIND THE PLEXIGLASS

"Just punch in the orders, and I will bag the food," Jeyja said.

"Wait a sec. I have to blow my nose quickly. Sorry," I said, rushing to the breakroom through the kitchen.

The kitchen staff was bustling and overflowed with people of all ages, their laughter echoing through the air. Some of the kitchen staff were yelling through their masks and face shields. About three people working in the storefront were quiet. Chase was communicating with Rolland in the kitchen and telling Rolland how many food orders they needed. Nessa and Lester were taking orders by the vestibule entrance door. A bunch of delivery drivers were waiting for food orders that were not ready when they entered the store.

When I returned to the online delivery area, I quickly punched the online orders. Jeyja was fast in bagging orders and bagged almost everything by herself.

Antonio said, "Nessa, can you tell the drivers to stay outside?"

Nessa quickly walked to the entrance door and asked the drivers to wait outside since the online deliveries were not ready yet.

"There's too many delivery drivers here. Don't let anyone come in." Antonio said to Nessa.

When I finished punching in the orders, I helped Jeyja bag them. One order left was missing a soup.

"Here's the soup. Take it." Macy said in the kitchen while making another big orders.

I rushed to the kitchen and grabbed the soup that Macy had made. Any day that would get my life in trouble was made that day; on a busy day when everyone was panicking to make the food orders, I dropped the soup! I looked at Macy, and she looked away.

"Oh my gosh! I'm so sorry, Macy!" I said apologetically.

"It's okay, just clean it and make another one, Macy," Antonio said.

Macy didn't look at me and didn't say anything. She continued making soups, and asked Rolland what else they needed in the front. My heart beat faster, and my hands started to shake. I felt bad for dropping the soups.

"How many burgers do you guys need?" Jennica asked me.

I didn't answer Jennica since I had a lot of things on my mind. I couldn't check how many burgers did we need. I ignored her. Jennica went to the online delivery area to check the receipts herself and counted the burger orders we required.

"How long for the order?" The delivery man without a mask asked me.

I didn't bother asking him to wear his mask since he had been waiting for the order to finish for fifteen minutes.

"I'm sorry, I dropped the soup, but we're making a new one," I told the delivery driver, and he looked pissed.

"Really?!" He snapped.

Macy made the soup quickly, put it in the bag, and said, "It's ready."

I said, "Thank you, Macy! Sorry!"

I gave the food ordered to the delivery driver, and he left quickly. Antonio helped the counter staff and checked the line outside the store.

Then Antonio said, "Rainna, go on your break, and Chase will cover for you."

I went to the breakroom quickly. I never realized how tired I was until I sat down. The adrenaline rush in my body was slowly going down. I drank water, and I felt exhaustion weighing heavily on my shoulders. Despite trying to keep my emotions together, I could no longer keep them inside. I was overwhelmed by my feelings; tears streamed down my face as I felt weak. I went to the staff washroom quickly. I wiped down my tears and blew my nose. I washed my hands thoroughly, returned to the breakroom, and used my phone to search for COVID-19 symptoms and where I could get myself tested.

'How would I tell my mom about having COVID-19 symptoms?' I thought.

In the evening, while my mom was washing the dishes, my grandmother was on her bed watching TV in the living room. I was sitting on our stairs, staring blankly, wondering how I would tell my mom I needed to get tested for coronavirus. My cat went up to me and asked for food since she was showing a gesture of bumping her head on my legs and meowing a couple of times.

As I waited for my mom to finish washing the dishes, I felt a nagging sensation in my stomach, and I boldly said to my mom, "I think I need to get a PCR done."

My mom paused, turned off the faucet, turned to me and asked, "Why?"

"Uhmm, because I have symptoms. And, uhm, they said that one of our co-workers caught the virus, and that worker had worked with me, and we bumped each other many times."

I spoke again before my mother could say anything, "but I was wearing a double mask and face shield and washed my hands many times."

My mother said, "So the virus had entered the house!" Her eyes widened, and she repeated her words.

Before I spoke a word, my mother left the kitchen and went to the living room. I fed my cat, went to the living room, and told my mom, "I'm going to the hospital nearby to get PCR done."

My mother asked, "Do you need to book an appointment?"

"No, it's walk-in," said I.

"Okay, go for it and let us know right away. Don't come near grandma." Mom said.

I nodded and went up to my room. I checked my phone and replied to my friends's messages on social media. I checked their social media stories, and my cat came into my room; she knew how to open the door. I searched for COVID-19 symptoms, including cough, fever, runny nose, difficulty breathing, and loss of smell and taste. I had a runny nose and cough, but COVID-19 would not affect my body for two weeks after catching it.

'What if I get a fever tomorrow?' I thought.

I went downstairs to find some chocolates and see if I still had a taste. I opened the sanitizer from my bag and smelled it; I still had a sense of smell. I found a chocolate bar in the fridge and ate it; I still had a sense of taste.

'Now, let's see tomorrow.' I thought.

I brushed my teeth and took a hot shower. I have read on social media that a hot shower is one of the best remedies to fight COVID-19 because it would temporarily ease COVID-19 in the body.

Before I sleep that night, I prayed earnestly. I was fully aware that this was one of my problems as a Christian; I only prayed and thought of God when I needed Him, but despite that, I prayed to Him.

"Lord, I pray that if I have caught COVID, heal me right away, and I pray that the virus won't spread throughout this house. Please protect my family, in Jesus Name, Amen."

The next day, I had a 10:00 morning shift; I woke up and went to work 15 minutes early. I was waiting in the breakroom uncomfortably, and I waited for Antonio to come in at 11:00, but at that time, he came in half an hour early.

"Hi Antonio, can I please talk to you?" I asked Antonio.

"Yeah, sure." He said. I entered the office, and he closed the door, and only he and I were in the office.

"uhmm, I think... I caught the virus," I said in a low voice, but he heard it.

"Do you have symptoms?" He asked.

"Wait," I ran out of the office and up to the bathroom to blow my nose. I sneezed a couple of times and blew my nose again. I washed my hands with soap and water, and when I went outside, I used my sanitizer to double-cleanse my hands. I went back to the office and talked to Antonio.

"Sorry, I have a runny nose and could not control it. I'm feeling weak right now, and I sneeze a lot."

"Do you have any family members who have symptoms?" he asked, and I said, "No. It's just me."

"How many people are there in your family?"

"We're five people living in my house," I said.

"Okay, you can go to the nearest hospital, and I will ask Jeyja to come in early, okay?"

"Now?" I asked.

"No, next year." He said sarcastically.

"Okay, Antonio, thank you so much," I said laughingly.

I felt relieved that I was not going to work, but I feared for my health and my family.

'What if I caught the virus? Will it end my life?' I thought.

Walking to the bus stop 700 metres from our workplace, I checked the bus schedule. I had to walk through the vast parking lot to the bus stop. Walking through the parking lot, I looked for a car resembling *Mariano's*. I didn't want to see him; if I ever saw him, I would ignore him. I walked faster and was glad I didn't see him or any car resembling his.

I messaged Jeyja and told her I was going to the local hospital. I also told my dad I'll get my PCR done. My dad lived in the Philippines and updated us on the situation there. They also kept track of the cases they had.

I rode two buses for 40 minutes to get to the hospital from the fast-food. When I arrived, the security guard wearing a mask by the hospital entrance approached me and asked, "For a COVID test?"

I nodded.

"Go to that building," said he, pointing to the other side of the hospital.

"Which one?" I asked.

"You see the red stop sign there? There, you see the blue Toyota that just drove past the building? That building," said he, pointing to the building where I was supposed to go.

Then, I said, "Okay, thank you!"

They had a separate building for COVID-19 testing. They were strict and wouldn't let anyone come to the hospital unless it was badly needed. Upon entering the building for COVID19 testing, I had to change my mask; they provided a new one for us, and no visitor was allowed. We had to sit on a chair that was 6 ft apart. All the hospital staff was wearing complete Personal Protecting Equipment or P.P.E. It was the same as what I saw on social media: they were covered with full P.P.E. I filled out the form and answered questions about my symptoms. It took me half an hour in the waiting room, and they would call us by our name for triage.

When they called my name, three hospital staff stood at the door inside the building and said, "Follow me." I didn't know who was talking. I followed the male hospital staff to where he was going, and somebody called me from the opposite direction. A female nurse waved at me, indicating that I should follow her. I got confused by their voices. Another hospital staff was there and asked me repeated questions about whether I had close contact with someone who tested positive and what my symptoms were, if I had fever or feeling nauseous.

I said, "I have runny nose, and closed contact with someone positive for covid."

A hospital staff was sanitizing the pens; each used pen, and I had to put my health card in a tiny basket so that my hand wouldn't touch the nurse doing triage. Another nurse approached me and led me to a room resembling a bedroom. There was a stretcher bed, a wood cabinet, a computer, and a chair for me to sit in. It took me half an hour to enter the room to chat with a doctor through Skype.

"I don't think you have COVID, Rainna. If you don't feel nauseous or vomiting at all, I don't think you have COVID." The doctor said through Skype.

She also said a lot of things I couldn't hear.

"Okay," I said, nodding.

I had no idea what was happening, and I thought they wouldn't do COVID19 test on me. The nurse was preparing something on the table, and kept sanitizing her hands with gloves.

The nurse sat on a chair in front of me and said, "Hold your sneeze, and when I take it out, cover your mouth with a mask."

'*Oh, so, we're gonna do the test*,' I thought.

I feared what those big cotton buds look-alike would feel in my nostrils. The COVID-19 test they have had looked like a wooden stick with some cotton on one end.

The nurse said, "I will take a sample from your mouth. Remove your mask, then look up at the ceiling. I will put the swab until this half of the stick to your nose."

The swab was about 2 metres long. I removed my mask and looked up at the ceiling. I opened my mouth, and the nurse shoved the COVID-19 swab into it. Then, she scooped the swab through my left nostril for about ten seconds. I wasn't sure if it was the same swab used on my mouth, but the tester stick felt like it itched and rubbed my brain, which hurt at the end of my nostril.

I sneezed, and cough.

"Cover your mouth with your mask!" The nurse said angrily.

I didn't mind her being angry. I knew it was hard, and they also needed to stay safe. I had teary eyes afterwards, and then I sneezed again. The nurse looked at me sharply; she looked tired.

She said, "You can use the sanitizer, and I will go out first, and then you go."

She gave me another mask, and I threw the old ones I sneezed on. I sanitized my hands and put a new mask on. The nurse sanitized her hands with gloves, removed her face shield and put on a new one. I noticed she wore an N95 mask and another disposable mask underneath N95. I wondered how the hospital staff could breathe through those masks.

Before the nurse left, she said, "You have to isolate yourself, even when you are negative for 14 days. I am unsure when your result will be available, but you can check it online."

She handed me a pamphlet with self-isolating instructions and a website to check my results. Then, I left the hospital and went to the nearest bus stop. I checked my phone and turned on my data internet to check my social media and to let Jeyja and Antonio know about my COVID-19 test experience. They said they would keep it a secret from the crew. I didn't understand why they had to keep it a secret from everyone at work.

I thought to myself that having COVID-19 symptoms was a blessing in disguise because I would have to miss work for two weeks. I wouldn't have to fear going to work to see *Mariano*. It was a relief that I wouldn't have to work for two weeks, yet I feared that I might have caught the virus. I feared that my family would catch the virus from me, and I feared my grandmother's health, who lived with us.

When I got home, I took precautions. I followed the pamphlets they gave me about self-isolating.

The isolation instruction includes:

- Do not share a washroom with anyone
- Use the same plate, utensils, and mugs for eating and let no one use them but you.
- Separate your laundry from others.
- Use a mask when going to the washroom.

I had to let my family know about my situation and that I would have to isolate myself and use a separate bathroom. I stayed in my room until

I got my results. My mother would bring me food and beverages. She brought me a mask, sanitizers, vitamins, fruits, and everything I needed. It sucks that I couldn't use our home gym and post my home workout on social media. I watched movies and series on Netflix, whatever shows that interest me. I would message Bruno as usual and talk to people online.

I messaged Bruno about my situation that I went for COVID-19 test.

My brother brought me an iced coffee and left it outside my room the next day. He knocked on my door and said, "ALAY" which means offering, sacrifice and giving as a gift. We laughed about it for hours because he was not supposed to enter my room, so he had to leave my iced coffee outside my room on the floor, and I would take it when he left.

Three days later, I got the result and tested negative. However, I still had to isolate for a couple of days since I had close contact with someone positive for COVID-19. I then cleaned my room and the washroom and sprayed them with antibacterial spray. Since it was spring and sunny, I opened the windows in my room and our bathroom. I felt great for testing negative. I messaged Bruno and sent him a picture that I had tested negative.

I was still isolated for a couple more days, as the doctor advised me to do since I contacted someone positive.

I was always energized at home since I could do many things, but one of the things I became fond of was online shopping. My brother and I would receive an Amazon package every single day.

"The delivery guy soon's gonna say 'this house again?' HAHAHA!" I said to my brother, and we burst into laughter.

He said jokingly. "Ew, get back to your room; you're still isolating."

It might not be great to have COVID-19 symptoms during the rise of the coronavirus spread, but it led me to stay at home for weeks and avoid *Mariano*. I realized that time that bad things happen for a reason; perhaps God saved me from any worse things that could happen that time with *Mariano*. If I hadn't have gotten any COVID-19 symptoms, I wouldn't have to take a break, but I did, and it was a way *to avoid Mariano* and to get past the gossip about us.

25

BACK TO WORK

Before I had COVID-19 symptoms, I found out that *Mariano* had a wife and three children living under the same roof. I could not care less about them since I was never interested in *Mariano* and had my Bruno with me. Bruno held my heart, and I loved him. But things escalated quickly at work, and people loved gossip. I had no idea that my co-workers had been talking about me and that I had an affair with *Mariano.* Making me look like a home wrecker, but I could not control what my co-workers wanted to think about me.

Antonio spoke to me privately at work and asked me questions about *Mariano* since he had been hearing a lot of gossip, and I told Antonio everything.

I said, "I only asked Mariano for a ride because I couldn't use my Uber, but nothing happened between us."

Antonio asked, "How many times did he give you a ride?"

I said, "About 2–3 times."

Antonio asked, "Did you hear anything from his wife?"

I said, "Yes, she called me a home wrecker."

"I have screenshots of *Mariano* and the wife's text messages that I can show you. I told him not to text me, but he still texted me." I said to Antonio.

When Antonio spoke to me that night, I prayed hard to God to deliver me from that situation. I never thought I would have been a topic at work, and they have talked about false allegations. I never would have thought I'd be called a home wrecker when I didn't do anything to the family.

When I was taking a month's break since I had COVID-19 symptoms and despite having negative results, I still had to isolate for fourteen days, but I stayed longer than two weeks.

When I was isolated for fourteen days, Antonio messaged me and asked me to write an incident report about what happened between me and *Mariano*.

"Do I need to write in a letter form?" I asked Antonio since I had no idea what the incident report was for.

I had begun writing with curse words. I was overwhelmed by my anger, my emotions bubbling up inside me like a pressure cooker. I could not stop the voices in my head, and I wondered what my co-workers were talking about me.

'What did they say about me? Am I good in the story?' I thought.

I then wrote a three-pages incident report about what had happened and the text messages *Mariano* had sent me. In the incident report, I also admitted that I was at fault for asking *Mariano* for a ride home.

After a month off, I returned to work, and I haven't heard anything from Antonio since I sent the incident report.

'Is there still any gossip about me?' I thought.

When I returned, it was a busy day. I wore the hairnet and rushed to the breakroom, hoping *Mariano* was not there. I looked around the kitchen area, but I could not see him.

One of my co-workers, two years younger than me, said jokingly, "Your first day today, Rainna?"

Then, I laughingly said, "Yeah, it's my first day!"

It was a joke, as if it was my first time joining the team after I had been off for a month. I placed my bag on the shelf in the breakroom. I walked up to the front store, and I started taking orders. There were new faces at work, and some team members went back, including Charles, who later dated Kathy.

"Hi, how are you?" Charles said, which caught me off guard because no one at work would ask how it was going.

"I'm good, thanks, yourself?" I said.

I didn't hear what he said because I was busy stocking up and waiting for management to tell me about *Mariano*. When I returned, it was a busy day.

'Nothing has changed; so far, it is still busy,' I thought.

As I bagged the online delivery orders, Jeyja stood behind me and said, "Welcome back!"

I said jokingly to Jeyja, "I regret coming back."

I found out that Jeyja was promoted to supervisor, and the management team had been training her.

Then, *Mariano* came, and two district managers in higher positions than our manager were in the kitchen. I felt it in my gut that they would talk to *Mariano*. I overheard someone in the office asking for my incident report. They all read what I wrote in the letter.

Then, *Mariano* went to the breakroom. I pretended to be busy with online delivery orders even though I only had one order, and Jeyja helped me with the orders. The office room's door was closed, and Antonio asked for *Mariano*.

"Where's *Mariano*?" Antonio asked, walking around the front of the store.

I looked up at Antonio, but he wasn't looking at me.

'*He was just there in the kitchen earlier,*' I thought.

My co-worker, Messy, called *Mariano* in the breakroom.

"*Mariano*! Antonio was calling you." Messy yelled. Messy was one of my co-workers, and he was funny, and his voice was loud.

Mariano dashed to the front store, and I accidentally looked at *Mariano*, locked eyes, and looked away when I was going to wash my hands. He always looked at me, and it felt uncomfortable. I felt like I had committed some crime against *Mariano* since I wrote an incident report about him and was against him. There were about four people in the office, and they talked for about an hour until I took my break. I was in the breakroom, eating my lunch from home.

Messy teased me, "Wow! Eating healthy foods, Rainna, what?"

"Just eggs and cucumbers," I said shyly.

Then *Mariano* came to the break room. *Mariano* and Messy were close friends.

"They're letting me go. Termination." *Mariano* said to Messy.

"Oh no. So this is your last day?" Messy asked *Mariano*.

"Yeah. My last day. Take care, guys, okay? I'll miss you all." Mariano answered.

I didn't look to see *Mariano* speaking. I didn't want to see him ever again. Still, deep inside me, I felt terrible for him because he had lost his job, and I knew that our manager, Antonio, would need a new supervisor like *Mariano*, who was good with technology. But I knew it was for good. Despite what other people thought of me, I'm glad I didn't quit the job.

One of the supervisors, Josiah, asked me what happened between *Mariano* and me.

"I don't know where to begin," I said.

"You are the second victim." Josiah said.

My eyes widened, and I was shocked, "Wait, what? For real?" I said.

Josiah said that I was the second victim, and that made me feel at ease, but it didn't change the fact that I was the victim, yet I was called the "home wrecker."

'As if I'm gonna like someone like Mariano, like even if he wasn't married, and I wasn't madly inlove with Bruno, I wouldn't still like Mariano,' I thought. I didn't break a family, yet I was called a home-wrecker at twenty-one.

Part

III

SECOND WAVE BEGUN TO BUILD UP

July 2020- December 2020

26

ONLINE COLLEGE SCHOOL

I went back to school during the pandemic to study. In 2020, I pushed myself out of my comfort zone, thinking, "What if this is my last day?" I applied to a College near me in Mississauga. I took a Medical Laboratory Technician/Assistant program. I knew it was worth going to college, and I couldn't live with only a high school diploma and work at fast food. There is nothing wrong with having only a high school diploma and working at fast food, but life is too short not to try new things. I also quit the job that stresses me out in the office. I also realized that life is too short to stay at a job where I am unhappy.

One of my co-workers, Macy, took the same program and was also in my class. Neither Macy nor I had backgrounds in the medical field, which we chose to study. It was hard for us to catch up, especially for her, since it was her first time going to a school in Canada. Macy was my only friend in college, the only one I would rant to when I was depressed about school. I had gone through trenches with Macy, especially during college, and I wouldn't have been able to survive without her.

I felt ashamed somehow, thinking I should be an excellent example to Macy since she was younger than me. I should have shown her the courage to study. But I couldn't even fill myself, and learning was complex. Studying was like a war within me because I knew I should be studying, but I couldn't understand my college teacher, and I constantly got distracted by the things and people at home. As much as I wanted to get my college diploma within a year, I could not keep up with a fast-paced study.

I was failing all my exams. I often struggled with exams; it wasn't just a one-time occurrence. There were opportunities to retake the tests at my school, so I consistently had to take advantage of this provision. During our lectures, our college instructor, Simon, would send us notes through Microsoft Teams, and when I downloaded them, the words were all jumbled. Besides, I was using a MacBook and didn't have Microsoft Word. I used Pages, and if I had to send something for class, I would have to convert Pages to Word format so that Simon could open it in the same format.

I felt a lack of motivation to make the necessary effort to succeed. This led me to question whether pursuing a medical career was right for me. While I harboured a strong desire to pursue writing, I also felt drawn to exploring other potential career paths.

I knew a few people from fast food who took nursing and quit their jobs because they needed to focus on studying and to protect themselves from catching the virus. Our job at fast food could have been helping since we were getting a minimum wage with a lot of work. We couldn't even study during our half-hour break because our bodies needed to relax.

One day, my MacBook didn't turn on. The place where I could get it fixed needed an appointment. I had to call Apple customer service, and they helped me turn it on, but it didn't work. They advised me to go to the nearest Apple store to get it fixed.

I checked online, and it said I needed to book an appointment since we couldn't just go to the store without an appointment. I booked a week from the day I booked the appointment. It was the nearest day I could book an appointment since the days were fully booked.

I had to use my mother's laptop for the online class and my friend's computer for my assignment. It was difficult, and technical issues stressed me out because I was not good with technology.

The line was long when I got to the Apple store to get my MacBook fixed. A lady who works for Apple Store asked me if I had booked an appointment and led me to where I should line up. She spoke to me loudly since the store was a bit loud, and only 15 people could come in the store. They had created a line outside the store for us to wait until someone from inside went out. Everyone had to wear a mask. The Apple store also had a red circle sticker on the floor, indicating social distancing.

I didn't have to wait long since I booked an appointment with them. My MacBook needed an update, and we waited for it to be updated and charged fully. After a while, my MacBook was fixed, and I cannot wait to use it again.

It was strange to see people inside the Apple store. They were wearing masks, and I noticed that most customers had hand sanitizer dangling on their handbags and backpacks.

After six months of schooling online, we had to practice our skills hands-on. There were about 18 or 20 people in the class, and they had to divide us into two because we were not allowed to be together in the room, which was considered too crowded. They had assigned us to be in A and B classes, and our school schedule was alternate. Macy and I were in the same class, A class. Class A went to school first, and we talked about what it was like to be in school for the first time; we briefly discussed what we would expect during our hands-on training. Then, the next day was class B, and the class A was off. As much as I wanted to have that kind of schedule for not going to school every day, I felt lazy and struggled with low mood and depression.

One of our classmates asked Macy and me, "Why didn't you guys choose nursing? It is a good career path, and you guys are so young!"

I said, "I don't like studying, so nursing is not for me, nor everyone."

"True, true," said Macy.

"This program is hard enough for me; what more of a nursing program?" I said.

Some days, I would bring my MacBook to work to try and study during my lunch break, but that never happened. My MacBook only added weight to my bag. As I sat down in our lunch room, I would stretch my legs while sitting down and stretch my arms up high. I would stare blankly at the wall. Some days, I couldn't eat because my body felt full, but my body was exhausted and could not function. Whenever I took my break, I wanted to rest, and I didn't want to study since I wouldn't remember any of it, and reading the unorganized notes that our college teacher gave us made learning more challenging.

Some of my classmates said that they had trouble reading the notes that Simon had sent us, even the ones with Microsoft Word. Macy and I were both struggling, and we tried working while studying to make ends meet, but the college program we took required more time. We shouldn't have been working to focus on studying, but we didn't have a choice.

'I shouldn't have gone to college during the pandemic,' I thought.

For a half-hour break at work, I sometimes just drank water, sat in a chair, and checked my phone. The hours passed without me reading my notes. *'What's the point of reading my notes if I can't understand anything?'* I thought.

Months passed quickly, and we had completed our in-person class, where we could practice on our hands. I was not ready to finish college because I had never learned anything. I was lost in life then, and I felt like I had made a mistake in choosing the school. It was a fast-paced study, and I was not a fast learner. I should have thought things through, but I didn't know better.

Perhaps it was a great thought to return to college and invest money in knowledge and skills, but I didn't have enough discipline to study harder. I couldn't understand any of my notes since they were disorganized. *'Maybe in another multi-universe, I would study again, but that time, I wouldn't choose a fast-paced learning college or go back to college during a pandemic.'* I thought.

27

ENTITLED CUSTOMERS

One day, we ran out of fries. Aside from mashed potatoes and salad, our fries were the most popular side for the combo. We had a lot of food orders from both in-person and online orders, and of course, we ran out of fries occasionally.

The customer was pleasant and ordered five combos of burgers, fries, and drinks. Our fries were enough for her order, so we made another batch, which would take seven minutes to cook.

I took the next customer after the big orders. She ordered a burger combo and wanted fries for her side.

"Hi, I'm sorry we just ran out of fries. Someone ordered a bunch of fries, and we ran out. Is it okay for you to wait?" I asked the customer nervously.

I explained the situation, letting them know I appreciated their patience as I worked to assist them as quickly as possible. I adjusted my mask and face shield to calm myself because I felt like a tightrope walker without a safety net. I felt like I needed to move when I was feeling nervous. I had been traumatized by people who yelled at me or us for not meeting their expectations of having the food quickly, fresh and hot foods. Luckily, the customer was friendly, and they were willing to wait for the fries.

Then, I served the next customer, who ordered the same thing but only one combo for himself. I told the customer that our fries were still cooking and that his order would take about five more minutes.

"You guys don't have fries?" The customer asked.

I answered him, "We have, but we're still making it,"

"That's ridiculous. What side do you guys have other than fries?" He asked.

"We have mashed potato and salad." Said I.

"That sucks, man! I only came here for the fries! I don't even wanna get a combo." Said he.

He removed his mask, and was sweating from wearing a mask.

"Sorry," I said, without meaning it. *'If you wanna complain, then complain. I hope you leave sooner,'* I thought.

He said, "I always come here every day and get my order ready. Holy smoke. Did you get a manager back there?"

"Yeah, I'll call him," Said I.

"Make it fast!" Said he.

I went to the office and called Antonio, "Hi Antonio, somebody wants to speak with you."

"Who?" He asked.

"The customer," I said.

"Why? What happened?" He asked.

I said, "The customer says he didn't want to wait for the fries, and he always comes here and gets his order ready and fast."

Antonio walked to the customer and talked to him. I checked the cooking time for the fries, and it says 3 minutes. The customer was ridiculed for complaining about waiting for the fries.

'If he has time to complain, he has time to wait. D*mbf*ck,' I thought.

"Yow, I think the customer is gay, eh? Can't believe he would complain about waiting for the fries and would like to speak with the manager." I said to Jan in the kitchen.

"Haha. Ask him if he was gay," said Jan jokingly.

"Maybe he's on his period," Chris said.

We all laughed in the kitchen. I walked up to the counter to inform the other customers that the fries would take two more minutes. They didn't mind waiting too long since they were also busy on the phone.

The fries were almost finished, and Antonio said the customer was okay waiting for the fries.

"It was unnecessary to call for the manager as if the fries would have been prepared faster if they had complained," I told Chris and Jan. Antonio went to the office, and he seemed pretty busy.

When the fries were done, I quickly put them in their container box and burned my finger a bit on the hot shelves. I gave the customer's order, and the customer was complaining and said,

"Sorry about the wait."

Then, the customer nodded and left the store.

28

BLACK SOCKS ONLY

Antonio would have sent someone without black socks and work hats.

I had a morning shift on a weekend and slept through the alarm as usual; I rushed to prepare for work.

As I rushed in, I wore my uniform but couldn't find any black socks. I thought, *'You know what, it's gonna be busy today, and Antonio won't even notice.'*. I'm 5'0 feet tall, and my work pants were slightly longer than my legs, so my socks won't even show. Before leaving the house, I always had sanitizer and an extra disposable mask. I rushed to put the mask on my face, and its loops broke. I got pressured to get upstairs to my room to get another one. I then took an Uber since I had no time to catch the bus. While waiting for my Uber ride, I made a coffee quickly since I couldn't function at work without coffee.

When I arrived at work, the first voice I heard was, of course, Antonio's. He asked the team member if the customer's order was ready.

I wore my hairnet as quickly as possible, walked through the kitchen, dropped my bag where there was a space in the breakroom lockers, and then proceeded to work on a busy morning.

The phone kept ringing nonstop, and there were a lot of people outside of the store lining up. The kitchen staff were yelling at each other because they couldn't hear each other and had to prepare a lot of food.

"Why is it so busy today?" One of the kitchen staff said.

"Well, it's the weekend. What do we expect?" I said.

"People should stay at home and protect themselves." Another kitchen staff said.

It was so busy that we couldn't even talk to each other at work. I wanted to talk to Chase about Bruno messaging me "good night," but we were swamped by work. We couldn't even go on break together because one person had to stay.

When I went on my half-hour break, I sat on a chair, crossed my legs, and lifted my pants slightly. Antonio went to the break room to use the washroom and noticed my white sock.

Antonio said, "Rainna, what are you wearing?"

Looking down my shoes.

"Did you know about the uniform policy? We should always wear black socks for work," said he.

I didn't know what to say because I knew I was in trouble for not wearing black socks.

Then he said, "Next time I catch you not wearing black socks, I will send you home."

I nodded, didn't say anything and used my phone. I felt terrified and irritated because why would they send someone home for not wearing black socks and not following the uniform policy? I had thought, *'Would not wearing black socks affect the profit and how we perform at work?'*. I didn't want to say anything to Antonio because it wouldn't make sense to him.

Then, he went to the kitchen and asked Nelia to check each team member's socks. Half of us weren't wearing black socks, so it turned out that it wasn't only me.

"Next time, I will send people home who aren't wearing black socks, " Antonio said, using the megaphone.

All my black socks were in the unwashed laundry basket, and I didn't have time to put them in the washer. Since then, I have checked if Antonio is scheduled on days I will be working so I can wear black socks. *'There is no way you would mind us not wearing black socks when we are doing the right job.'* I thought.

29

MY WORK HAT

I saw Jeyja throwing a water bottle once, but it was still in good condition.

I said, "You're throwing that out? They might come back for it."

Jeyja said, "Yeah, Antonio said throw it out since it's been there for a while. We are not allowed to leave things here in the break room."

Since then, as much as I wanted to bring my water bottle, I would keep it in my bag, but most of the time, I'd get bottled water from work, which needed to be punched in and paid for. We couldn't just take food and drinks without punching them in and paying for them.

Most of the time, I left some of my stuff at work. Sometimes, I forget my hair tie, eyelash curler, and hand cream in the washroom. I even forgot my old phone once. Some of my co-workers, even Jeyja, were nice enough to keep the stuff I had forgotten and give it to me the next day because if a supervisor saw a team member's staff in the break room or the washroom, they would throw them out. I felt privileged to have Jeyja as my work best friend because she is close to Antonio, and she was very nice. I relied on Jeyja a lot, especially at work.

One night, I was rushing home to catch my bus when I left my work hat in the washroom. I felt a nag in my heart, and I could not stop thinking about my work hat.

I thought, *'It's a work hat, they won't throw it out.'*

Antonio would send us home if we didn't have a hat because it was the company's uniform policy.

I texted Jeyja and asked, "Are you still at store?"

Jeyja replied, "Yeah I am, why?"

I replied, "Can you do me a favour, please? Can you check the washroom and check if my work hat is still there. I forgot it in the washroom."

"There is no hat here," Said Jeyja.

My heart beat so fast that I got nervous. I got home, showered, and felt uncomfortable about losing my hat. I hoped it would be in my bag, but I checked it, and the hat was not there. I couldn't sleep appropriately since I kept thinking about my work hat.

When I went to work the next day, I checked the washroom first, but my hat wasn't there. I told Antonio my work hat was missing, so I put on a hairnet and worked. Antonio could not suspend me for not having a hat since we were short-staffed. I lost my hat and knew I had left it on top of the box in the washroom beside the shelves. Someone from the afternoon shift must have taken it.

Rolland said, "What happened to your head, Rainna?"

"Huh?" I was confused about his question.

"Where's your hat?" Said he.

"Somewhere over the rainbow," I said jokingly, and we laughed.

Then I said, "I left it in the washroom yesterday, and now it's gone."

"We'll be getting more uniforms by next week, and I'll give you a new hat," Antonio said.

"New hat that you can lose again, *Ateng*!" Rolland said jokingly.

We all burst into laughing.

Then Jeyja asked the other team members if they needed replacement pants for their old ones. Some of the team members' zipper pants were broken. She wrote a list, and some of them needed a new uniform.

"I need a new uniform, both pants and the top uniform; I gained weight," my coworkers told Jeyja. Then Jeyja wrote them down.

It was awkward taking the customer's order without a hat on. I looked like a guy with pink eyeglasses on.

When it was quiet, I tried looking for my work hat, hoping it would still be there. Boldly, I asked the team members in the back if they had ever stolen it. Of course, they all said no.

"You should have put a name on your hat," Lester said.

"Yeah. Well, I'm not going to stay here longer. So." I lifted my shoulders and pouted my lips

"True, true." He said.

I worked for four days without a hat. I didn't figure out who stole it. Since I have a huge forehead, I felt exposed way too much without the hat, but thankfully, Antonio gave me a brand-new work hat that I could never misplace again.

Days later, our new uniforms arrived. My co-workers who had ordered new uniforms were happy to get a new one.

"Rainna, here's your hat. Lose it again, okay?" Antonio said sarcastically, handing me a new hat.

Jeyja and Rolland overheard what Antonio said, and they laughed. We all laughed.

"Oh, perfect! Thank you so much!" I said excitedly.

"Later, she would lose that again." Said Rolland, referring to the fact that I would lose the new hat.

I said, "Yeah, I'll leave it in the washroom again. Haha."

I felt light-hearted, realizing that even when we were tired at work, we still had a place in our hearts to laugh about silly things. Even in the most challenging times, it was great that we still continued to laugh about small things. We goofed around when there were no customers, and it made me feel that working at a fast-food restaurant during the pandemic was worth it. I got a chance to laugh with my co-workers and socialize with them. I also got free and discounted food after my shift. I realized that even in the most challenging times, we can still see the beauty in every ugly situation.

30

BAD DAYS

"Life is difficult, and everyone has bad days. Everyone has trouble because it doesn't matter how rich you are; sickness, trouble, worry, and love will mess with you at every level of life."—Domhnall Gleeson.

We ran out of chicken, but a batch was coming up. The chicken takes about 20 minutes to cook in a deep fryer. Some days, only one person was breading and cooking the chicken, which took a lot of time. Mostly, the supervisors had to multitask and help the people in the back speed up the chicken breading process.

A customer approached me and asked, "How long will it take for my order?" Although they wore masks, their foreheads were frowned upon, and I could see the frustrations in their eyes.

Once the order is cashed out and paid for, two receipts come from the receipt machine: one for the customer and the other for the people who prepare the ordered food. I was responsible for letting the kitchen supervisor know how many chickens we needed for the order, but I didn't check our receipts. I didn't work proactively to avoid such a situation.

Many trays were on the counter where we prepared the order, and many receipts were coming out. Ralph asked Chase to stop taking orders for a while because many people were standing and waiting for their orders to be done.

"How long will it take for my order? Tomorrow?" The customer asked angrily.

I was shocked by his voice and turned to look at him. He looked like he was in his 50s and carrying a child about four years old. I wasn't sure if it was his child, nephew, or grandchild. But I wish he had set an excellent example for the child to be friendly to the fast-food workers.

"It would take about ten more minutes, sir," said I.

I never wanted to apologize because I knew they would still yell at me, and it would not change the situation that they would have to wait for their orders for a longer time.

As for me, apologizing was a sign of weakness because I would show my vulnerability. I didn't want to say "sorry" without meaning it. I didn't see the reason to apologize for making them wait, though I needed to because I was in customer service. I turned my back to them. I couldn't handle their frustration, especially myself.

I didn't want to show them I was weak. To cope with such a situation, I would toss the trays in their place loudly and have tantrums. Every sentence I spoke had curse words. I didn't want to feel weak, and I didn't want to show I was not okay. I didn't want to lose myself because I would have raged and fought the customers if I did.

Another two customers came up to the counter and asked how long will it take for their orders since they had been waiting for a while. We also got a lot of online deliveries, and the driver deliveries were waiting for their order.

"Excuse me!! Order for this one," said the delivery driver, showing me his phone with the customer's name.

"That is not ready yet," I said, and I hid in the delivery area.

"I can't breathe with a mask on!" The delivery driver said. "Can you do it quickly?" He raised his voice.

I asked Ralph, "Ralph, how long will it take for the chicken?"

"It's ready," said Ralph.

We finished the orders, and the customers left. Some delivery drivers cancelled the orders because they had been waiting for the food for too long.

When it slowed down, I realized that the customers who yelled at me didn't know me, and I didn't know them. There were still good customers who were patient and were understanding about our shortcomings, and I'm grateful for them.

Another incident occurred when I returned from my break on the same day. Bill, Lester, and Chase were talking while waiting for the food items from the kitchen, and I was taking the customer's big order. A customer asked for 15 pieces of chicken and 15 burgers. With big orders like this, I would always repeat and ensure I punched in correctly.

I said to the customer, "I'm going to repeat the order, sir, so 15 pieces of fried chicken with gravy and 15 orders of burgers,"

The customer was looking at me dead. He didn't respond, and he was ready to pay for the order using his credit card.

"Will that be all?" I asked for a confirmation.

He said, "Yeah."

He didn't even confirm if what I said was correct. I gave the total, and he paid for it. We prepared his order for about 15 minutes. Then, the customer took his orders and left. He came back again after ten minutes and asked me for his drinks.

"Hi, something is missing from my order. You forgot my drinks," he said angrily. Everyone was looking at him.

"You didn't order drinks," I said.

"Yes, the f*ck I did! You guys are just talking and talking and not paying attention to the customer." He said with a strong Filipino accent.

I was waiting for him to laugh. I thought he was kidding. *'He can't be serious.'* I thought. I was looking at him as if I saw a ghost.

Then he said, "Give me the drink!"

I said, "Sir, I repeated your order and asked if that was everything, and you said, 'Yeah.'"

One of my pet peeves is when someone blames me for the wrong things I didn't do. I did my job perfectly fine. I ensured I got everything he asked for, and then he would come and look for items he didn't ask for and pay for.

He then checked his receipt and saw that the drinks had yet to be punched in and paid for. He asked me how much our soft drinks were, and I said, "It's about two dollars each."

"Two dollars for a drink?" He asked.

"Yeah," I said.

He left the store without buying the drink.

I exclaimed, "Are you kidding me!?"

Then I went to the dining room near the entrance door, where the guy went through. I saw him walking towards his car.

"What was his problem?" Antonio asked.

"He was asking for his drinks, which he didn't pay for. It's okay that he left already." I said.

Another customer complained that the fried chicken had blood and didn't cook well.

The customer approached me and said, "Hi, there is blood in my chicken. Would you please give me another one?"

The customer was polite. I gave her another piece of chicken and asked,

"Do you need anything else?"

She said, "No, I don't need anything else. Thank you so much."

"No problem," said I.

One of my colleagues, Marsha, in the burger station area saw what I did.

Marsha asked me, "Did you tell the supervisor?"

She was talking about the lady complaining about the chicken with blood in it.

I said, "No. Why would I tell the supervisor if I could just replace it with another one?"

Perhaps she was shocked that I said that. I didn't want to bother any supervisor since they were busy and have worked so hard, and if there were things I could easily do, I would do it.

"Are you dumb? You have to tell the supervisor. You can't just give them on your own." she said, giving me a dirty look.

I said, "Okay, I will tell Antonio."

Then I went to the office and told Antonio what had happened.

I said to Antonio, "There was a customer who complained about the chicken with blood. She was polite and friendly though. I gave her a new chicken and asked if she needed anything else, but she said that was it."

"It's okay. Where is the customer?" Antonio asked.

"She's eating somewhere in the dining room. But she's not even mad." I answered.

"Oh, okay," said he.

Then I left the office, walked to the burger station, and talked to Marsha.

I said to Marsha, "I already told Antonio about the customer who complained about the chicken,"

Marsha looked at me, said nothing, and continued making burger patties. Since then, I have never wanted to talk to her and have not been fond of working with her. She seemed to have a bad temper and was careless. I went to the break room to drink water and remove my mask. It was hot, and the mask was itchy.

'It is just a bad day and not a bad life.' I thought.

I still enjoyed going to work because it distracted me from what was happening in the world. I laughed with my co-workers at things we found funny, and we all forgot about the pandemic. I cherished every moment with my co-workers; although sometimes we had misunderstandings and bad days, we still had each other's backs during the pandemic.

In the afternoon they assigned me to prepare food orders. I was trying to be as fast as possible because I took pride in working at another fast-food restaurant for five years and becoming the quickest worker among my co-workers back then. I quickly assembled the orders and dropped one food item on the floor. Everyone looked at me, and I felt mortified.

Chase asked, "Are you okay?"

"Yeah. No. I don't know," said I, looking down on the floor.

I took the food from the floor and cleaned it immediately. Everyone was staring at me.

A few minutes later, they assigned me to the bagging area and placed Charles and Chase in my position as an assembler of the food. They were both fast. I had felt some way where I wanted to disappear because I felt ashamed.

'Can I just disappear now?' I thought.

I wanted to disappear at that moment. I wanted to be like bubbles that everyone could poke and suddenly disappear. I wished the ground would eat me whole. I worked on autopilot again. I felt terrible because I thought I was replaceable and needed to be better at work.

"Let's go outside for break, and take extra minute" Naveena said.

"Yeah, I'm down," I said, excitedly.

"Let's go, bro. Hurry up!" She said.

As I finish bagging the orders, I said, "We're not allowed to go on break together though, haha,"

"They won't notice!" Said she.

"Right." I answered.

We went outside the fast food restaurant on our breaks. We talked about how funny the customers and our co-workers were and talked about a lot of gossip while walking down the sidewalk. We laughed loudly by the restaurant's corner. We would always go outside during our break. We weren't allowed to go on break together, but we did. We would take an extra five minutes of break before returning to work, and the management never noticed.

Everytime we worked in the afternoon, we would wait for each other to finish work to hang out together after work. When we finished work, we went to the plaza near our place and took pictures with funny filters on social media.

"Remove your mask!" Naveena said.

I was scared of removing my mask since I didn't want to catch the virus, and I had a lot of acne. Naveena was the kind of person who was fearless and a person that I could be open with.

Then, I said, "I don't want to, I have a lot of pimple."

"We can put filters," Naveena said.

I removed my mask and threw it to the garbage can near us. We took pictures of ourselves and said,

"Let's do fierce pose!"

Naveena looked fiercely and put her hand on my shoulder. I made a wacky face pose, bit my lower lip, closed my eyes, raised my eyebrows and smiled. We burst into laughter again, and some people in the car laughed at us. We loved taking pictures for memories and laughter. The photos we took would always be on my phone, and I would post them on her birthdays.

We crossed the road again and found a place to sit down. "Bro, we looked like homeless people," I said.

"Let's take a picture again, looking like a homeless person." She said.

"We need a Timmies cup and a sign asking for donations. HAHAHA!" I said jokingly, "I'm going to be homeless instead of working at fast food. HAHAHA!"

Then, we talked about our *situationships*. *Situationship* is a relationship without a commitment or considering themselves as a couple. Her having a situationship with a man, and I have a situationship with Bruno. We've got some teas to share about the guys we were talking to.

"I missed Bruno, bro. He's so handsome!" I said.

"You always talk about him. Forget about Bruno. He doesn't care about you." She said.

I always talk about Bruno, how handsome he is, and how I missed seeing him before the pandemic. We went to another fast-food and bought some food.

"I'm gonna take an UBER, how about you?" Naveena asked me.

"I'm gonna take the bus; it's before eleven o'clock," I said.

"Nah, let's go, I'll pay for your UBER." She said.

"Bro, are you serious?" I said.

"Yeah. Put your address here."

"Thanks, bro!" I said.

A few minutes later, while we were in the car, I looked through the car window and realized that even on bad days, I could still be grateful for the little things I had. I have a good friend right there. I have a job I didn't like, but the best people I have met so far were from the fast food. Naveena was a rare gem; she had no idea how grateful I was that night with her.

At the end of the day, I also realized that we all have 24 hours in a day, and we can do something to improve our day by staying calm and remembering that everything will come to pass. Perhaps my 7-hour shifts didn't go as planned, and it was a bad day; I still had myself. I would go home, shower, play with my cat and write in the corner of my beautiful home. I would do the things I love, and none of the bad experiences that happened that day would linger in my mind.

> *"You have to remember that the hard days make you stronger. The bad days make you realize what a good day is; if you never had any bad days, you would never have that sense of accomplishment"—Aly Raisman.*

31

CYSTIC ACNE

"For many people, stress can be a trigger for acne—and we are certainly living in stressful times," said Dr. Julia Carroll, a Toronto-based dermatologist at Compass Dermatology.

Acne flare-ups were common during the pandemic for essential workers and those who stayed at home because a stress hormone, cortisol, can lead to acne flare-ups.

During the pandemic, many individuals experienced increased acne flare-ups, particularly essential workers who faced heightened stress levels in their jobs and those who remained at home isolated and full of uncertainty in life. Everyone seemed stressed during the pandemic, and a stress hormone, cortisol, had led to acne flare-ups.

Cortisol is a stress hormone that helps initiate the adaptive "fight-or-flight" response to stress. Cortisol can lead to inflammation and stimulate the production of oils in the skin, both of which can exacerbate acne conditions. As a result, many people saw their skin health deteriorate during this chaotic time.

I could not breathe with a disposable mask and face shield. It was itchy and uncomfortable to use. I had no health reasons to put off wearing a mask, but I had no choice. I didn't want to catch the virus, and my grandma lived with us at home. Older adults are prone to getting the virus quickly because they have weakened immune systems. I changed using a washable clothes mask so I could breathe.

One of my mistakes was not washing my reusable mask every day. I had many reusable masks, but our manager, Antonio, wanted us to use the black-coloured mask they provided for us.

Antonio said, "It is part of our uniform to wear a black mask and nothing else."

Then Antonio saw me wearing a white flowery reusable mask. We looked at each other. I was about to laugh, and he said,

"If I see someone wearing a flowery white reusable mask, I will send them home."

I laughed my arse off and said, "Can I go home?"

Antonio laughed, and he gave me the black-coloured reusable mask.

As of November 2020, I noticed three big pimples on my cheeks — two on my left cheek and one on my right cheek. I didn't usually get these kinds of acne, and I barely had acne breakouts. I only get pimples once a month during my menstrual period; it's called hormonal acne. But the hormonal acne didn't stay that long on my face.

As of December 2020, I got a massive acne breakout. It was itchier to wear the mask, and I never had to rub a pimple until I got the acne breakout. I was not too fond of it when I went to sleep, and when my body tried to relax, my acne wouldn't stop itching at night.

I posted my picture on Instagram and Facebook, letting people know that I was going through an acne breakout, and then some people started recommending products that helped them. I tried some acne products that my family and friends advised me, but nothing helped.

I was not eating correctly. Though I exercise regularly doing a home workout, I would fast before and after my home workout, and when I ate, my food intake was not a good source of nutrients that my body needed.

I would wash my bed sheets and pillows bi-weekly to prevent acne breakouts. If my theory was correct, dirty bed sheets and pillow covers were the primary cause of my acne breakouts, aside from wearing face masks. But the acne didn't disappear. I had felt more insecure and looked down on myself for having an acne breakout.

I had low self-esteem, and I would use camera filters to take pictures of myself to cover the pimples. My co-worker, Bill, said, "Stay away from make-up for a while, and let your face breathe." Which I did.

It was not just acne, but cystic acne. The pimples were big, red, itchy, and it felt uncomfortable. Sometimes, I would scratch them at night because I could not help it, and they would bleed. The softness I'd had on my face was gone; now, it felt like a bunch of stones and asteroids on my face, for it was hard, rough, and patchy.

Some of my friends said I was still looking beautiful with acne breakouts, but during those hard times, compliments meant nothing to me because I was battling and struggling inside my head, and I didn't want a massive acne breakout on my face. If my acne were gone, I would take their compliments.

I contacted my medical aesthetician, Roxy, and she recommended products to me. I trusted her since she shared many informative videos about acne and she studied for it. As a minimum-wage earner, the products were a little pricey for me, but I knew it would help me.

Two days after using the products Roxy recommended, I felt less itchy on my face. Then, three months later, I still had acne, but it healed up most of the acne. I saw that my face improved from the products Roxy had recommended. The itchiness was gone, but I still had breakouts and acne marks.

According to the National Library of Medicine, "During the COVID-19 pandemic, 45.35% of the participants reported that their acne complaints increased, 27.33% reported relapses and 7.56% reported occurrence for the first time. Newly formed acne was reported most frequently on the chin (78.26%)."

Everyone I knew has had acne flared up during the pandemic due to stress and wearing a mask constantly. Mask mandatories had destroyed our faces, and it cost us so much during the pandemic.

32

MENTAL HEALTH

In November 2020, I was diagnosed with mild depression and low mood. I was lost, heartbroken, and in debt. I stared at the ceiling into nothingness, contemplating my whole life and what I wanted to do. Since I couldn't understand anything in my online class, I watched some YouTube tutorials about the topics we discussed. A few hours later, I zoomed out, staring at my phone's screen.

'I don't feel like learning today.' I thought.

I then took a nap to rest my body. When I woke up after a few hours of sleeping in the afternoon, my body felt heavy, and even though I had taken some time to rest, my body was fatigued. My mother called me downstairs for dinner, but I didn't feel hungry. I had never eaten anything that day, and despite the delicious aromas from the kitchen, I found it hard to muster any appetite for the meal.

'I have to do my assignment.' I thought.

My mind was fogged with jumbled thoughts. I knew I had a lot of things to do, yet I couldn't fathom which one to prioritize first. The weight of my thoughts pressed down on my chest, making it harder for me to breathe.

My mental health was deteriorating. My work shifts were only on Fridays, Saturdays, and Sundays. I didn't get a chance to study the school materials because my body was tired of working in a fast-paced environment. I had to keep my body moving and do some work chores when we didn't have customers.

We had to keep our masks and gloves on while working, and it added stress to me, thinking that what if those masks and gloves weren't safe enough to protect me and my co-workers?

When I tried to study at work, I was constantly distracted by the people who talked to me in the break room. The break room was small, and we had a few lockers. There was only a table and about five chairs. Some of my co-workers would go outside for breaks or spend their free time inside their cars. We weren't allowed to sit in the dining area because it was closed, and customers might complain when they saw us sitting there.

I experienced a lot of stress during the pandemic, especially while in college. At first, I enjoyed my online college class, but then we got a new college teacher on theory, and everything became dull while the cold months were approaching. I didn't have the energy to listen to my college teacher through the screen. I didn't expect online classes to be dull; the college teacher only read the papers, and I struggled with his teaching style because I am a visual learner. I didn't learn anything from just listening from a laptop.

Our college teacher then would put himself on mute during break time, but we still had to be online. We can end the call if needed, but we must go back online at a specific time. I asked my college teacher, during our break time online, if the school offered free counselling because I was depressed about everything that was happening in my life. He told me that I could ask my physician to help me since the school wasn't offering any counselling at the moment. I thought that my college teacher was joking around by telling me to ask my family physician to help me with my depression. It was my first time being depressed. I mean, I got sad and felt all negative emotions, but I have never felt the way I felt when I got depressed during the pandemic.

I didn't have enough income because I was in college and drowning in debt. I had to focus on studying, but depression, anxiety, and low mood hit me like a ton of bricks. I couldn't even escape from the sadness I was feeling. I felt like a chain was pulling me from achieving my goals.

My college teacher has helped me somehow, and I am thankful for that. I contacted my family physician just in case my college teacher was right, but I thought my family physician couldn't help. However, my family doctor did help me. My family physician sent me some websites I can visit online and phone numbers to call. I contacted the public health and the websites she has given me, but I was still not sure if that would help me deal with my depression. It was hard for me to accept that I couldn't afford a therapist, but I was lucky enough to live where I live because I found a public health service that offers free counselling.

33

THERAPY

I found free online counselling, and I had a therapist named Julia. I told Julia everything that was happening with my life, and tears fell down my cheeks as I typed them down. My hands shook, and tears were all over my laptop keyboard cover.

My heart shattered for Bruno, for realizing that he was not in love with me the way I thought he was. I found it more challenging to work as a cashier while my heart was ripping apart, and it took a toll on my mental health.

I was insecure because I had acne on my face. I had an acne breakout, and I've never experienced it before. I'd only get pimples here and there during my menstrual cycle. My face broke out with cystic acne due to stress, anxiety, and wearing a mask while working.

I also needed to catch up with schoolwork. I was still determining where I would start with a workload. I would sleep during an online class. I never wanted to study; I only wanted to snuggle in my blanket and watch Hallmark movies.

I was stressed about my finances since I only worked weekends starting in July 2020. I was a minimum wage earner. Although I knew I needed to save and spend wisely, I was stressed out due to my workload and the fear of catching COVID-19. To cope with stress, I spent a lot of time online shopping. Everything was closed, and there was nowhere to go, so online shopping became my hobby and stress reliever.

My therapist, Julia, said "depression is useless."

She didn't mean to say that my depression and feelings weren't valid. She pointed out that if I stay depressed, then it is futile. I wasted my time overthinking, I wasted my time trying to control things I couldn't control, and I merely focused on what I felt.

Julia added, "You must act based on your goals, not your feelings."

She sent me a lot of articles to read about mental health and wellness and gave me some helpful worksheets to complete and advice. Through worksheets, I have learned many things. Most of the worksheet I had to do was self-reflection. I learned more about my emotions and became aware of who I was and what I could be.

I thought that since the online therapy was for free, they wouldn't give me the full benefit of getting out of my depression. When I told Julia everything, I expected her to solve my problems for me. But she was there to help me solve my problems, and I still had to allow myself to overcome my depression.

Social media is also taking a toll on my mental health. I saw people doing better while living in the same world I lived in during the pandemic. I saw people hitting a home workout, and they have progressed. I saw people starting new hobbies and finishing a book. I had seen them all on social media and could not help but compare myself. Thinking about not being good enough over and over again would not save me time over nonsense thinking.

Bruno, who broke my heart, has saved me from being with the wrong person. He told me that he couldn't love me the way I deserved to be loved, which broke my heart, but it certainly saved me. It hurt me, but at least he was honest about it. I learned to stop thinking about the things I couldn't control. I couldn't control or change the form of his heart into loving me. It was out of my control. But I kept thinking about it back then, and I couldn't stop thinking when I rejected the guys around me and ignored them for this guy I fell in love with. In the end, I got heartbroken.

I learned that overthinking will not solve a problem. It would only make the situation worse. I was overthinking about the future. Will I get married one day? Would I want to change my career path? I overthink way too much. To cope with my overthinking, I would watch movies and sleep. When I woke up, I'd repeatedly stare at the ceiling blankly. It was a waste of time for me because I didn't do anything that much in life. I have wasted my time when I could just be happy and do the things that matter.

I was not motivated to study, so I did what my therapist told me to do: prioritize my goal instead of what I felt. I reviewed three chapters in three nights. Though I felt weak and tired, I did what she said. Learning can be tedious, and I wasn't a fast learner or someone who got A+ or 90s on report cards.

Studying three chapters and deciding not to pay attention to my feelings helped me. When I achieved my goal, I rewarded myself. I snuggled in my blanket, watched Hallmark movies, and felt lazy again, but at least I had accomplished something.

Julia said, "Depression is not just a feeling. It is a mental illness. But if you are continuously hating yourself and criticizing yourself and are not going to help yourself, nothing will happen. Perhaps your depression would get worse."

I was helpless and lost, and I felt like I couldn't move from one place to another. But I reached out for help. I contacted my teacher, my family physician, and the public health access available online. I didn't want to stay in a gloomy place without life where depression was trying to pull me.

After three months of online therapy sessions with Julia, I beat my depression. I survived depression by believing that I could beat my depression by changing the way I think and approach life and also being with God with me. I outlived it because I prayed to God in the Name of Jesus Christ for healing and help. I have survived because I spoke to a professional therapist and could stand up on my own feet again. I realized during this challenging time that having a therapist as a Christian is okay because being a Christian does not mean we are perfectly fine. Believing in Jesus Christ does not mean we are exempted from the sufferings in the world. We get depression and anxiety as well, just like others. We are not perfect human beings, and we have shortcomings as well. I prayed to God to help me cope with my depression because it was hard for me. When I prayed to God and talked to my therapist, there was a light in my heart. I knew there was hope. We are not alone in this chaos; we don't have to walk alone because we are created to help each other, and therapists are there to help us. I learned that mental health is as important as physical health. The pandemic reminded us of how precious our mental health is, and we have neglected it by eating poorly manufactured food. If we don't take care of our health, we will, of course, get sick.

34

BLOOD WORK

The beginning of the year 2020 has changed a lot. I remember when I was walking down the sidewalk to get to the bus stop to work, I thought I shouldn't have to worry about coronavirus since it was only in China. Little did I know that was the last time I didn't have to wear a mask anywhere I went. Little did I know the coronavirus would significantly impact everyone's life.

Getting our blood work done during the pandemic was a luxury. I felt terrible for older adults who were not tech-savvy because everything should be done online, and not everyone had a computer or smartphone to book online appointments. It was okay for me and others with smartphones to book ahead. It took a lot of work to save a spot and find availability for blood work.

As requested by my family physician, I needed to get my blood work done for an annual check-up, but I had to book it somewhere else and not at the clinic where my family doctor was. I had to wait two weeks for the appointment at the blood work location near me since it was the only date available.

Two weeks later, I went to my blood work appointment. There was a clinic staff by the entrance, and before entering the clinic, I had to change my disposable mask to a new one that they would provide and sanitize my hands. There were signs on their entrance door about COVID-19 and how to book online for an appointment since they weren't taking anyone by walk-in. Everyone had to book an appointment online, and they wouldn't let anyone who didn't book an appointment.

Before entering the clinic, they would check the temperature of everyone who comes in, and they would ask questions such as:

- Do you have symptoms such as runny nose, cough, or diarrhea?
- Have you been told that you have to isolate for 14 days?
- Have you been contacted with someone positive for COVID-19 for the last five days?

I answered "no" to all of the questions. Then, they told me to sit in the waiting area. We had to sit six chairs apart, and they wouldn't let anyone enter the Blood Test Clinic until someone got up from the waiting area seat. The front desk counter had plexiglass, and the staff wore complete Personal Protective Equipment (P.P.E). They wore gowns, N95 masks, a face shield, and a head covering. It was hard to hear them when they were calling our names to be seated in the room where they performed blood tests.

I heard this saying: "Health is wealth," but I never knew what it meant until the pandemic hit and learned that we wouldn't appreciate our health until we ate hospital foods and stayed in the hospital for too long. We wouldn't appreciate our health until it was our time to get sick and can't move.

As COVID-19 cases increased, I saw other countries go into lockdowns. People started gathering in grocery stores, forming long lines so they could enter and buy everything they needed because they feared it might be the last time they could buy outside. People started wearing masks everywhere they went; the death rates from COVID-19 were going up, and some of my co-workers resigned due to COVID-19; it made me believe this is the end of the world. I was paranoid, worried and scared. But there is a thread of hope, and I held onto it.

Hope is something that people shouldn't lose. I found hope in eating healthy foods and doing exercise. I discovered we can all beat the coronavirus if we strengthen our immune systems. Every day, I would eat oranges and take Vitamin C. I would eat fruits and exercise daily. I needed to be healthy because I had a grandmother living with me. My family lives with me, and I work at a fast-food restaurant six days a week. I thought and was determined I couldn't catch the virus and bring it to my family. I have to be healthy.

When it was my turn to get my blood drawn, the Lab Technician was pleasant and didn't have difficulty finding my veins. I drank more water before my appointment and didn't need to fast for my blood test.

When I finished my blood work, I asked the front desk staff, "When do I get the blood test results?"

"Sorry. What?" The staff said.

I paused for a while, thinking I used the wrong wording.

"Until when would I wait for the…. results?… Of my bloo…."

The staff cut me off, looked into my eyes, and mumbled. I didn't understand what she said, and they seemed pretty busy.

"Okay. Thank you." I said and left.

Usually, they would send the test result to my family doctor, and if there were anything wrong with my blood result, my family doctor would contact me to discuss it with her.

35

UBER RIDES

My life as a fast-food worker was both tedious and fun. It was boring when I was not at work, and it was fun when I was at work. At home, I would scroll on social media for hours and read some books sometimes. I could not go out because there was no way to go, and some parks were closed.

Due to the pandemic shutdown, most establishments were closed, and I could only socialize at work. Although I was not too fond of the job and some people I worked with, I enjoyed socializing with my work friends. Our work was only fun if we worked with the people close to us because it made it easier and more fun.

One morning, I slept through my alarm clock and woke up half an hour before my shift started. I checked my phone's notifications first to see if Bruno had messaged me, but he didn't text me.

'Oh my gosh, I'm so in love with Bruno.' I thought.

I had to rush to the bathroom and take a quick shower. I had to brush my teeth while in the shower to make it easier. That took me about ten minutes, and I fed my cat. I called Uber because there was no way I would be there on time if I took the bus.

My brother asked me when my work would start, and I said, "At 12."

"You should be more responsible; your Uber won't take you to work faster," my brother said.

That hit me hard to the core. I was stunned to speak because he was right. I need to be more responsible for waking up on time because Uber would not reach my destination faster, and there might be traffic and accidents.

When I called for an Uber, it took 4 minutes for the Uber to pick me up. We also had to wear masks inside the Uber car. Most Uber cars had sanitizers available, and some had masks for the passengers. The Uber car had plastic covers between the driver and passenger seats. We were only allowed to sit behind the driver's seat, and only one or two people were allowed as passengers as long as the two people were together and lived in the same house. Uber could not take any more people due to the distancing protocol. Unlike before the pandemic, Uber drivers could bring more people simultaneously and drop them off at different booked destinations. The Uber driver arrived ten minutes before my shift started.

The Uber driver, Maria, was friendly and asked me if I was on my way to work.

I said, "Yes, I'm on my way to work. I start at 12."

I was hoping that she would drive faster to get there by 12. I didn't have to worry about the traffic because the roads were empty, and only a few cars were on the road. Drivers still had to follow the traffic lights, and Maria stopped by the red traffic light near the gas station.

She said, "Gas prices are down, but there's nowhere to go."

"I know, right? Even the flight prices are like 15 dollars," I said.

"Yeah, it's crazy," said she.

We stopped talking, and Maria went on when the lights turned green. I avoided talking to UBER drivers as much as possible because I wanted to enjoy the few minutes I spent sitting in a car before work.

Then, Maria talked again. She asked where I worked, and I said,

"At fast food. To where we are going"

"How is it working there?" She asked.

"Oh, don't ask. Haha. It's unbelievable, and it's different now. The customers are more brutal now than ever. I used to work at another fast food restaurant for five years until pre-pandemic, and of course, some customers were rude too, but now, the customers are wild and more brutal. They didn't wear a mask, and we were the ones that would get in trouble." I said.

"That is crazy! I know. My son used to work at a fast-food restaurant, but now he works in the office at home."

"Oh. He works from home." I said.

"Yeah, I do Uber now because I got laid off." She said in a sad voice.

"Oh, sorry about that. Hopefully it gets better." I said.

"Yeah, I don't know when this will stop, but you do good. You know, work and work, and don't stress yourself out. I know my son did the same, but I can't imagine, you know, it's just uh, don't take it personally," she said.

"Yeah, and some customers would yell at me for waiting a long time, but we get a lot of orders, too. One customer last week yelled at me because she had been waiting for 20 minutes, so, like, chill, you're not the only customer here." I said.

"Yeah. That's crazy!" She said. "You do good, get paid, and go home."

"Yep, that's the way," I said.

"Yeah, I know. It's hard, but you can do good." She continued talking. "But take rest too. This is what I tell my son. You need to eat well and rest. Your body needs some uh, rest, and you know some uh."

"Nutrients," I said.

"Yeah, and vitamins." She said.

Then, we arrived at work five minutes late for my shift.

"Yeah. Well, it was nice talking to you. Thank you so much. Take care!" I said.

"Thank you, Bye!" she said.

I exited her car. I felt relieved for sharing some stories about work, but I somehow felt uneasy about opening up to her. *'But she's a mother, she would understand,'* I thought.

When I entered the store, it was busy with online orders. *'Ugh, I should've called in sick.'* I thought.

During the pandemic, the need for emotional support skyrocketed as people grappled with isolation, anxiety, and loss. My Uber driver, Maria, went above and beyond to comfort me as her passenger. It was about a 15-minute ride, but she offered a listening ear, engaging in heartfelt conversations with those who needed it most like me. Maria offered encouragement and empathy as I poured out my frustrations and fears. Her genuine care and compassion transformed her car into a safe space, providing a sanctuary for people like me and not just a ride.

Antonio was busy and didn't notice I was about five minutes late. "Rainna, do the bagging. We have a lot of online orders." Antonio said, and I did as he asked me to.

Antonio had an attitude where he wouldn't ask people how they were doing or even say hi; he would put me where they needed me. But if I work with my work friends, I wouldn't mind Antonio.

I had the same weekend shift from 12:00 to 20:00, and two people called in sick. No one would want to work because they knew it was not worth working on a weekend. The weekend was the busiest, especially in the afternoon and lasted until night when we closed.

Antonio asked me if I could stay until closing. I said, "Yeah, I can stay until closing."

"Okay." He said. Without saying 'thank you.'

I felt unappreciated, and I somehow regretted staying until closing. I was young, and perhaps I was strong enough to work more hours, but my mental health was deteriorating.

'Really? You can't even say 'thank you' to your employees?' I said in the back of my head.

Chase worked a closing shift, usually from three o'clock to closing time, which was nine o'clock at night. However, we had to stay an hour more to clean up the store. We changed our closing times many times during the pandemic.

I told Chase, "Listen, Antonio can't even say 'thank you' when he asked me to stay until closing, but I'm glad you're here, Chase!" I giggled.

"Awww, girl!! Don't mind him." Chase said, and they patted my shoulder.

When I worked from another fast-food workplace, they would show gratitude towards me, especially right after my shift. I had no doubt that's why I stayed there for five years. I just had to quit that job because we moved to a different location, and I told myself I needed to expand my horizons. But I never thought I would land at another fast-food workplace that doesn't even appreciate me.

I said goodbye to Chase and the other workers a few hours later when we finished a horrible shift. I went to the office and said goodbye to Nelia.

Nelia said, "Bye Rain, thank you for today."

Nelia was the only supervisor who would appreciate everything I did. She was my favourite supervisor.

"Maybe you wanna stay here and help out cleaning," Antonio said, smiling.

"Hahaha, no, my cat is waiting for me, but I'll be here tomorrow," I said.

"Haha, okay, take care." He said.

I squinted my eyes at Antonio to pretend that I was smiling. They could not see my mouth because I was wearing a mask.

I booked an Uber ride for a dollar more at night. They increased the price for Uber rides because they were also essential, perhaps unheard of as crucial heroes.

The Uber arrived, and as I sat in the back seat, the driver, Patrick, asked how I was doing, but I didn't hear him. I could still hear Antonio's voice and noticed Patrick staring at me through the rearview mirror. I heard him mumbling, then realized he was talking to me.

"Oh! I'm so sorry I didn't hear you talking. I worked ten hours today, and it was crazy busy," I said apologetically.

"Oh, no worries! How was your day!?" Said he, with a loud voice.

"I'm tired and wanted to get home," said I.

"Oh no. You work at the fast-food place?" He asked.

I said, "Yeah, I wanted to quit, but bills kept piling up, so I can't complain."

Then he said, "Oh that sucks, eh? Well thank you for still working. I heard horrible stories about fast-food chain workers, and most people quit."

"Oh, yeah, I had a lot of co-workers that quit because the customers were mean to us, and we were still low-wage workers. And you know, some people looked at us as slaves," said I.

"Oh yeah, that's so true, eh? It sucks, but you gotta do what you gotta do." He said carefully.

I felt he wanted to say something, but he was careful.

I asked him, "Have you worked at fast food before?"

Then he said, "Yeah, but I only lasted for a week. Hahaha. I can't do work like that. You have to be fast."

"Yeah, you have to be fast and accurate, but right now, even though you are fast and give the people the right order, like the correct food they ordered, they would still complain. They complain about the protocols and the prices as if we were the ones who made them. Hahaha," I said laughing to ease the tension in my heart.

"Daaaangggg, that's awful! I'm sorry you had to go through that. Well, people are like, you know, they complain a lot." said he.

"Yeah, they complain just to complain," I said.

"Yep, that's true," said he.

As much as I didn't like talking to Uber drivers, drivers like Patrick and Maria healed me. They made me feel at peace for letting out what was inside my chest. Though it wasn't a long conversation, I felt at peace when I talked about what it felt like to be a fast-food worker during the pandemic.

The encounters between essential workers and Uber drivers showcase the support, appreciation, and understanding. The Uber drivers offer as they transport tireless individuals like me.

Amidst the chaos and uncertainty of the pandemic, Uber drivers continued to provide transportation services to those in need. While many people stayed home, essential workers still had to commute to their jobs. The Uber drivers understood the risks but chose to serve their community. They all took every precaution, wearing masks, sanitizing the car regularly, and even offering hand sanitizers, wipes, and masks to their passengers. Their dedication and commitment to keeping essential workers moving during challenging times earned them the gratitude and respect of those they transported. Although Uber drivers were somehow our emotional support and essential heroes, some UBER drivers still had terrible attitudes.

Part

IV

THE SECOND WAVE PEAKED IN MID-JANUARY 2021, THEN EASED.

36

MY HEART RIPPED

Whenever a family member of the crew passed away, our management would make a donation box for a worker to take as our help and ease the financial situation of the deceased family, except when my grandfather, in my dad's side, passed away in 2021. I have told them about my grandfather's passing. I posted about it on social media for my co-workers to see, and they have seen my post. Some of my co-workers messaged me, saying that they were offering their condolences to me.

However, despite my co-workers and some of the management team seeing my post, they didn't make a donation box for me. I wanted to ask them if they were still making a donation box, but I didn't want to come off as greedy.

'They prolly don't do it anymore.' I thought.

A few days later, one of my co-worker's grandparents also passed away. They made a donation box for her. It pained me deeply to see a coworker whose grandparent passed away, and the management team set up a donation box for her.

'What about me? My grandfather died too, just a few days before her grandparent died.' I thought. I never shared my feelings with anyone because I thought no one would understand my feelings.

A dark cloud of grief descended on me when my grandfather passed away. Memories of the times we shared flooded my mind. I was never close to my grandfather, but every time I visited him as a kid, he reminded me of my father, who was working abroad. They both had the same facial features, and my grandfather was the only one I could see physically resembling my dad.

Despite the weight of my emotions, I found it challenging to shed tears. I was lost in deeply reflecting on my grandfather's life and impact on mine. The last time I saw him was before we migrated to Canada in 2013, and I never saw him again.

'This is so unfair!' I thought. *'It wasn't about the money; it's the thought that counts.'*

My heart ripped apart for the management team for not making a donation box for me like anyone else at work. I also worked hard and picked up shifts to cover even when I needed to rest. I felt unheard of. I just let it slide. I deactivated my social media for a while because Antonio would post something on social media about treating their co-workers like family. Yet, he didn't seem to care about workers genuinely. I get it, we all post a good thing on social media, sometimes to paint a good image of us, but the people who know us in person would know us even better.

I held some grudges for a while, which I knew was not the proper response when I was treated unequally, but I couldn't avoid it, and it was traumatizing. Later, I realized that holding some grudges would only put weight on my heart. I kept thinking and saying positive words whenever I thought about how unfairly they treated me.

I kept thinking positive thoughts and learned to let them go by accepting that no workplace is perfect. Nobody is perfect. I still stayed and worked for them, and I still worked the way I worked. I told myself that it was okay and I was not that important to them, not as important as my other co-workers, which was okay. I didn't have to argue for the donation box, argue for a "most favourite employee" list, or do something to make them like me.

That was something I took to my heart. I got hurt for not being treated fairly. Perhaps the management didn't like me because of some issues I had with *Mariano*. I got involved and was the victim, yet it showed that I was not. Perhaps they didn't see me work hard enough. Maybe I was too emotional to be working at a fast-food restaurant. Possibly, they didn't mean to hurt me like that. Whatever the reason, my experience has taught me to forgive and not just let it slide but actually to forgive and let go of the grudges.

37

"I'M NOT COMING BACK HERE ANYMORE"

I started cleaning the counter at storefront for closing, filling the cups and plastic bags with no customers in the line. Some of my co-workers were talking while cleaning, and some were in the office, asking for time requests off.

Two of my co-workers started cleaning the dining area, and Jan was mopping the floor already.

'Isn't it too early to mop the floors?' I thought.

Then, half an hour before we closed the store, a customer came in and ordered a lot of food and drinks. My newly hired co-worker, Amy, was taking the order. Amy was only 15 years old and had no work experience, but she was a good worker.

When she took the customer's order, we made them immediately because we were closing and wanted to finish cleaning as soon as possible.

While preparing the customer's order, I briefly talked with Jeyja. "I'm so tired of work; why would the customer come here with a big order when we're closing, hahaha," I said, laughing my annoyance off.

"It's okay, we're almost there!" Said Jeyja and patted my shoulder.

I loved working with Jeyja. We worked well together and knew what we were doing at work. However, sometimes, she had to correct me if I needed to do something differently or use an incorrect method at work.

We gave them the customer's order and locked the door. We started cleaning up and throwing everything out except the soups. I considered taking them home instead of throwing them out, but I had to ask Antonio if I could. My co-workers in the kitchen cleaned their area, and Amy and other workers cleaned the storefront.

I was cleaning my area in the kitchen, and then Jeyja said, "Guys, the last customer is knocking on the door." while she was looking at the CCTV monitor.

Jan opened the door for the customer to come in, and the customer rushed to the front and looked for Amy, who had taken her order. The customer threw the big plastic bag with her food item on the counter and said, "Where is the girl who took my order? This is not what I said I want."

Jeyja called Amy, who was in the break room on her phone. "Amy, come outside."

"Huh? Why?" Amy said.

"The customer is here to see you. Did you forget something?" Jeyja said to Amy.

Amy and Jeyja went to the front and talked to the customer. The customer said many things to Amy; I barely heard them. But I saw the customer's face without a mask. Her forehead frowned, her eyes were deep, and she bit her lips: "I need you to change my order. This is not what I asked for. You're not listening!"

"It's okay. You can go to the break room for now." Jeyja told Amy.

Amy cried in the break room. "What happened?" I asked Amy, but she couldn't speak.

"Do we still have soup? Did you throw them already?" Jeyja asked me.

"Uhmmm…no, not yet, but let me check." I checked, but we only have enough for one soup order.

"Yeah, but I think it's not enough. How many soups does she need?"

While waiting for her order, she rants about Amy for not listening carefully: "Now we must wait again just because the girl wasn't paying attention." The customer wanted the chicken, but Amy punched her order incorrectly. Instead of chicken, Amy punched burgers. When the customer returned, we had already thrown the chickens away and recorded them as waste.

"You can keep the burgers, Ma'am." Said Jeyja apologetically to the customer.

When we gave her soup, we also gave her free french fries as an apology. Then the customer said, "Thank you. I'm not coming back here anymore."

When the customer left, Jan had to mop the floors again. The customer had stepped on cleaned floors, and the customer's shoes were muddy, and the mud was stuck on the floor.

"Urgh! I have to clean the floors again." Jan said.

Jeyja locked the door. We talked about the customer and how mad she was. Although we knew we were at fault, the customer acted unreasonably like that and made our co-worker cry. Everyone makes mistakes, and we have a way to resolve the problem.

"Then don't come as if we want you here," I said.

Then my co-worker, who was washing her hands, said, "Right? As if she's important."

Then my other co-worker changed the garbage and said, "Don't come. We don't want you here."

We talked about the customers who weren't nice to us, especially those who made the workers cry. That was the only thing we could do: talk about them and judge their appearance.

"She's not pretty enough to complain like that," said my other co-worker.

"She could have said it nicely," I said.

That is how we cope with rude customers. We wanted to let it out because we would all burst out if we didn't.

When we left the store, I had to book an Uber. It was a quiet ride, and I couldn't stop thinking about my grandmother and everything that happened at work. I hated to see my co-workers getting yelled at by customers because I knew how it felt to get yelled at.

'It's so tiring.' I thought. *'Maybe the customer who came back last minute was going through something. Well, everyone is going through a lot these days. I don't know, but I am sososo tired.'*

I took a deep breath because I didn't want to cry during the Uber ride, but I felt heavy in my heart.

38

HOSPITAL VISIT

I was at work on a regular day when my mom and her friend rushed my grandmother to the hospital. My grandmother was in distress, complaining of pain, and she was visibly upset. It was a worrying situation, especially during the pandemic. My mother said to me that my grandmother didn't want to wear a mask, and she would remove it because it caused her discomfort and itchiness.

When my grandmother was admitted to the local hospital, my mom and I visited her on my day off. Additionally, due to the ongoing pandemic, we had to undergo COVID-19 testing and screening before being allowed inside the hospital. We also had to register as essential family members, proving our blood relation to my grandmother. Whenever we visited her, the hospital saved our names as her immediate family.

We also had to provide and show them our I.D. to check if we had the same address as my grandmother. Before we could enter the facility room, they had to ask us COVID-19-related questions: whether we had any COVID-19 symptoms, whether we had to be isolated for 14 days, and whether we had close contact with someone positive for coronavirus. We also had to change our masks, and if we were wearing a washable mask, we had to change them with the disposable mask they provided and sanitize our hands.

Navigating the hospital corridors felt like wandering through a maze, with strict protocols in place for visitors. We had to ask a few hospital staff members for directions to the unit where my grandmother was.

When we found my grandmother's room, upon entering her room, we were required to sanitize our hands and wear personal protective equipment (PPE) to minimize potential risks. The stringent measures in place were a stark reminder of the challenges and precautions necessary to protect loved ones during these difficult times. We spent a few hours in my grandmother's room, but we had to leave by nine in the evening as it was a limited-time visit. We weren't allowed to sleep in the hospital rooms, but unlike before the COVID-19 pandemic hit, we could sleep in the hospital with the patient. Indeed, everything has changed when the COVID-19 pandemic hit.

39

ANTONIO DISLIKED ME

Since *Mariano's* incident, I have felt uncomfortable with Antonio. I noticed how Antonio had changed his attitude toward me. He didn't greet me anymore or talk to me to ask me to do some work.

One afternoon shift, as I put on my hairnet and walked past the office, I greeted Antonio,

"Hi, Antonio."

He looked me in the eyes, ignored me and talked to my co-worker working in the kitchen. I brushed it off and thought he didn't hear me because of the mask covering my mouth.

The next day, I had the same shift. I greeted Antonio,

"Hi, Antonio. Is it busy today?"

I asked him and spoke to him a little bit louder—loud enough for him to hear through my mask. He looked at me and ignored me again. However, he greeted Bill, who was right behind me.

"Hi Bill, how are you today?" said Antonio.

"I'm good, thanks! How are you?" Said Bill.

I wore my hairnet and walked through the kitchen to put my bag in the break room. I felt a sting in my heart. I thought, *'What did I do for Antonio to ignore me?'*. Since then, it has been hard for me to talk to him, and I have not felt secure talking to him because he might ignore me again.

The following day, I observed him. I had a mid-shift that usually started at eleven o'clock in the morning and went on until four o'clock in the afternoon. We were busy that day, and it got busy when I was about to finish my shift. Antonio was looking at the schedule on the clipboard.

I walked to Antonio and said, "uhmm, my shift is done."

"Okay," said he.

He didn't look at me; he was looking at the schedule sheets. I expected him to ask me to stay for an hour or so because we had a line-up outside the store. He didn't bother asking me to stay. However, he asked one of my co-workers to wait another two hours since it was busy, and my co-worker did an entire eight-hour shift. I could have stayed as well, but he didn't ask me.

The following weekend, we again got busy with online delivery orders, phone calls, and in-store orders. Two people worked on each station—the burger-making and gravy stations. We had enough people to take online orders and operate the cash registers.

Before my shift ended, I boldly asked him if he wanted me to stay, and he said, "No, it's okay. You're tired. You can go home."

I said, "Okay."

I noticed that he only greeted non-Filipinos. I talked to Naveena about it, and she noticed it, too.

She said, "I'm not gonna greet him again; he doesn't even say 'hi'."

"He only greets non-filipino," I said.

"Right?! He doesn't like his race," Naveena said.

We were talking about Antonio in the breakroom. Then he came to use the washroom. I didn't greet him. He never looked into my eyes. I didn't have to ask him why he was ignoring me because his attitude was showing towards me. Naveena and I went outside instead of staying in the breakroom for our break.

On another afternoon shift, we had downtime. I looked for plastic bags and walked to where we put the trays. Antonio saw me walking towards the trays and said, "Why are the people in the front just standing? Just because there is no customer doesn't mean you will stand there."

He snapped. Seeing terror in his eyes, I drew back. I was one of many in the front. There were about four people, and yes, we were standing, but no, we were also doing some stuff.

Lester was going on break, waiting for his food. He won't do anything since he logged in during his break time. Chase was preparing the food for Lester. We weren't allowed to make food; somebody else had to prepare it. The other co-worker checked the fries to see if we had enough, and I was looking for plastic bags to stock up. Everyone was doing something at work. Then, Antonio yelled that we weren't doing anything from the kitchen. He assumed we were standing and chatting and not doing anything but didn't know or see what we were doing. Everyone was doing something on the front. But I felt uneasy when I caught him only looking at me.

'Why was he only looking at me?' I thought. I felt a hard pounding in my heart. I felt he hated me because *Mariano* got fired. *Mariano* was our "techy supervisor". He would fix stuff such as our cash registers and the computers in the office. Since then, Antonio had to do and fix every technology we have to fix.

That week was one of hell's weeks for me because I could tell that Antonio didn't like me for some reason. Not everyone will like each other, but it stung my heart to know that my manager didn't want me for some reason, and I had no idea why.

The fact that the management didn't make a donation box for me when my grandfather died despite telling them about my situation, Antonio despised me. He pretended to be busy in the office and didn't take the time to listen. Perhaps he listened to me, but he didn't care.

Then, early in 2022, I went out with Jeyja to drink and try new cocktails nearby. I heard that Antonio was playing favouritism at work, and I noticed that Jeyja was his favourite supervisor—everyone at work could tell that—and she was also a friend of mine. We went out because why not? We had been working a lot and wanted to celebrate our hard work. Also, I landed another full-time job and worked two full-time jobs. My back and head had been hurting for a while, so I wanted to take a moment and enjoy my life.

Jeyja and I went to the restaurant after work. When we got our drinks, we took pictures of them, which we posted online. We drank a lot of drinks, and I got drunk quickly. We took a photo while waiting for the Uber to arrive. We both looked buzzed, so we took an Uber home and got home safely.

Then, the next day, I called in sick.

Everyone knew, especially the supervisors and, of course, Antonio. They saw our post on Social Media. Adrianna said,

"Rainna got drunk, so she called in sick.".

They called me to the office the next day, after calling in sick, and Antonio talked to me.

"It looks bad that you are close to the supervisor, and your action was unacceptable." Said Antonio. Then he reran his mouth for 45 minutes, and then he said, "This is the last time you're going to do this."

I called in sick because of back pain and felt ill for weeks; I was okay working with a hangover. But that day, I just dropped my body. I was drained and sick for weeks since I worked two full-time jobs. I knew I was wrong. The management was okay with Jeyja since she was the supervisor, and perhaps they told her not to hang out with me anymore.

Ever since the incident with *Mariano*, I felt hated by the manager. Yes, we joked around and liked each other's posts on Facebook, but it altered my brain to think he hated me.

I learned to see good in every bad situation as a young adult. Especially during the pandemic, I learned to be grateful for my little things instead of complaining about what I didn't have. With Antonio, perhaps I was right that he didn't like me as a person and worker, but I am still grateful that he became my manager. Although I wouldn't say I liked his post about leadership and being a family at work because he was not a family and not a good leader to me, he was one of the reasons I got the job at the fast-food restaurant. He hired me because he saw potential in me.

Perhaps he hated me because I did things to be hated for. While riding the bus, I thought, *'Maybe if I didn't ask Mariano for a ride, nothing would happen, and he would still be working at the fast-food restaurant. Maybe it was not the case, but Mariano got fired because of me and through me. Perhaps Antonio wouldn't hold grudges toward me if I wasn't close to Jeyja and didn't drink with her.'*

When I got off the bus, I rushed to my place, showered, and wrote in my journal. I got teary-eyed as I was writing about Antonio for hating me. As I was writing a journal, I realized that not everyone will like me. I don't want everyone, either. I let Antonio hate me if that was the case. All I knew was that I needed to work and pay my bills. I knew I was not going to stay in that workplace. I also realized at that time that I shouldn't have any of my co-workers on my social media or post any personal life on social media.

40

THE INCREASED PRICES

In January 2021, the bus fare increased by CAD 0.25, which is an annual increase. The grocery price also increased, and so did the prices of our food items.

One morning, I served a customer who didn't want to wear a mask. Even though I wore a mask, I could still smell his foul breath from six feet away, with plexiglass between the cash register and the table in front of it.

"Hi sir, sorry, but you have to wear a mask upon entering the store, and we cannot serve you," I said to him politely.

It was hard to say things out loud because I talk slowly. I got frustrated seeing customers not wearing masks upon entering the store because, despite the pandemic being talked about for a year, some people didn't know or pretended that they didn't think we had to wear masks.

"Oh? I didn't know that," he said sarcastically. "Can you give me a…?"

I interrupted him and said, "Sir, you must wear a mask; otherwise, we cannot serve you."

I was ready to get my supervisor because he smelled like morning funky breath, and I couldn't take it. Sometimes, I wanted to talk back to the customers because they tested my patience.

"Just take my order; I don't have time to get a mask." He yapped.

"Okay, what can I get for you?" I said, knowing the supervisors would get mad at me for letting the customer order without a mask.

"Can I have the burger combo with fries and drink? That's it." He said loudly.

I appreciated people who knew how to order and what they were ordering because it speeds up the process. The transaction was fast, and I didn't have to ask the customer whether they wanted to make their order a combo.

"Okay, will that be all?" I asked the customer.

"Yes, and I'll pay by credit card." He said.

"Your total is sixteen dollars and fifty-eight cents," I said.

"Woah! That's expensive. Can you check carefully?" He said

I said, "An order of burgers with cheese, medium-sized fries, and a drink. Your total is sixteen dollars and fifty-eight cents with tax included. You can check the screen right here."

I pointed to the screen on the cash monitor where customers can see their orders being punched in. He reviewed his order carefully.

"Just a burger combo, right?" He said.

"Yes, just a burger combo," I answered.

Since he was taking longer to check his order, I prepared his drink.

Then, he asked, "Why is it so expensive now? The last time I came here, it was only ten bucks. Why is it expensive?"

"They increased the price just like gas, bus fare, and grocery prices," I said while holding his drink.

"That is ridiculous." He shook his head no.

I didn't mind him if he didn't want to place an order anymore because I wanted him to leave. I wanted him out of the store because of his unpleasant smell. I understood that it was in the morning, and maybe he had just got out of bed and went straight to our store. Perhaps he had a medical condition, but I could not take the growing bacteria inside his mouth. Maybe his smell was typical for him, but not for me. My supervisor came in, Nelia, the most excellent supervisor, and said,

"Good morning, Rain."

Then he looked at the customer.

"Good morning, Nelia." I said.

"Okay, you know what? That's expensive. I'll pay by credit card," he said, deeply breathing.

This time, I walked to the office to smell something nice.

"Rain, the customer smells so bad," Nelia said.

"Right? He took time to order, too, and he didn't wanna wear a mask!" I said, then I walked to the front, and his card didn't go through.

"Sir, your card didn't go through," I told the customer.

"Oh, sorry, I'll pay cash." the customer said.

He paid the exact amount in cash. Then, I prepared his food.

"Do you need help, Rain?" Nelia asked. "Nope, I'm good. Thanks." I said.

I prepared his order as fast as I could. I made his burger and put fries in its box container like a wizard.

"Here you go, sir. Have a good day, and thank you!" I said.

I rolled my eyes and wiped the counter. Hoping that he didn't see my eyes rolling. I was going to remove my mask because I needed some air, but fear held me back. *What if there was a COVID-19 droplet around the store?* I thought. I wore a mask every day and barely removed it, even when using the washroom at work. I only removed my mask when I was eating.

41

THE GOOD CUSTOMERS

Despite dealing with complaints daily, there were still good customers who understood our situation. One afternoon, I was taking the order, and the newly hired supervisor was training in the kitchen. She didn't tell us that we were running out of chicken and that their orders would take twenty to thirty minutes to get ready.

I was taking this gentleman's order. He asked for fifteen pieces of chicken.

I said, "It's going to take about half an hour for your orders to make. I'm sorry about that."

My initial expectation was that he would get mad and not like waiting for half an hour for his order.

Then he said, "Yeah, that's fine! I'm going to come back in half an hour. Take your time." While squinting his eyes, I knew he was smiling behind his mask.

"Thank you so much, and here is your receipt," I said, handing him his receipt.

"Thank you, see you later." he waved me goodbye.

I felt light-hearted when a customer like him understood our situation. The fact that he would go outside and return later made it easier for us since there would be more space for people waiting for food inside. He didn't ask us why he needed to go outside and wait, unlike other customers who would ask us why they needed to return. It might have been a small gesture of respecting our policy, but it was more for us.

'Wow! There are still good people in this world.' I thought.

⁎⁎⁎

I was having a bad day, so I slammed the trays on the counter because three customers gave me an attitude. First, I asked the customer to wear a mask; otherwise, I wouldn't serve him, but he didn't want to and yelled at me because he just wanted to get his food. The second customer complained about the waiting time, and the third customer asked for mayonnaise, but we didn't have mayonnaise at the store. She kept telling me to go in the back to check as if going to the back would have mayonnaise magically.

My co-workers would not mind when we slammed the trays because we all knew we were having bad days. We always had at least one customer that pissed us off and would ruin our day. But I had to keep my cool and hold myself accountable.

Five customers have already placed their orders and are waiting for them to be made. They were all wearing masks; three stood while looking at our menu board, and two were on their phones. There were about eight people in the line, looking at the menu board, waiting to be served.

I have noticed that our customers avoided sitting on three chairs behind them in the waiting area, mainly because it was a pandemic, and they thought that the chairs weren't sanitized. They would rather stand than sit on the chair and catch the virus from sitting.

One of my co-workers, Bill, asked the customers waiting in the line to distance themselves and follow the red circle sticker indicating that they should stand 6 feet away from each other.

The online orders kept ringing, and we had about seven online orders. The people who worked in the kitchen were all busy and noisy. Rolland, the supervisor in the kitchen, dropped the thongs they used for chicken, and he had to run to get another one. Then, one of my co-workers in the kitchen asked where the thongs were because he needed to transfer the kitchen. Macy asked how many soups we needed because she would make more. Marsha asked if he needed to make more patties for the burgers.

Rolland's eyebrows scrunched together and said, "Yes! Just make more soups and burger patties! Wash the thongs right away and bring them here, please!"

"Good afternoon, welcome to our store; how may I help?" I said with a little wave to the customer.

The customer squinted his eyes as he walked to the counter. He knew our protocols since he stood behind the green tape on the floor. I squinted my eyes back but not smiling behind my mask.

"How are you today?" The customer asked me.

I didn't know what to say because I was having a bad day, but I guessed it was just a greeting.

"I'm good. Yourself?" I said.

"Are you sure you're good?" said the customer, laughing.

"Yeah, no. Actually, no, I'm not good at all. It has been busy today." I said.

"Oh, that's too bad. When do you finish?" said the customer.

"I still have two more hours, and I can't wait to go home and remove my mask," I said.

"I know it must have been difficult for you guys. Well, thank you so much for working." He said.

"Yeah, thank you." I almost cried. It was the time of the month when I was getting my hormonal emotions. Then I said, "What can I get for you?"

I took his orders, which were two burger combos. When I gave him his order, he said, "Take it easy, my friend."

"Thank you so much! Have a great day!" I said.

Standing behind the plexiglass counter during the bustling afternoon rush, I was shocked to find a customer who genuinely appreciated and understood us fast-food workers. It was a hectic afternoon, with orders coming in rapidly and the line stretching out the door. Most customers seemed focused on their phones, some looking at our menu board, eager to grab their food and go. However, some customers approached me with a friendly smile and initiated a conversation, wanting to chat in the middle of the chaos.

42

COLLEGE PLACEMENT

My college placement was taken at the clinic near my place. It was scheduled from Monday to Friday, 9:00 to 16:00, and I would go to work afterward. I had to take two buses from my college placement to work. My fast-food job schedule had changed since I started school and changed again when my placement started. My work schedule began at five o'clock in the afternoon and ended at ten o'clock in the evening on weekdays. I was still working full-time and had Mondays and Tuesdays off while doing my college placement.

On a non-busy day at my college placement, Melanie, the clinic manager, asked me to help her sort the papers and organize some papers in the clinic. Every paper had a date, and she asked me to throw away the 2015 papers.

I was sitting on the chair and organizing the papers. My eyelids were heavy, and I was trying to open my eyes since I was sleepy and tired from work. My clinic manager came in and asked me something I didn't hear. I didn't answer her. She left the room. Perhaps she saw me sleeping on a chair while pretending to organize the papers. I pushed myself and started organizing papers. She came in again with a bunch of disorganized papers.

"When you finish, we can start removing the papers on the board in the break room." She said.

"Okay," I said enthusiastically.

I pretended that I was okay, but my body wanted to rest. Melanie noticed that I didn't want to work, but I wanted to work and help them out as much as possible, but I was fatigued. I just wanted to nap since my body and mind were tired. I was not paid for my hours with them since I technically paid them to train me. Although it was needed for college, I didn't feel like working hard for my placement.

During downtime, we had to sanitize the chairs and entrance door handles. Every patient that comes in for their appointment must call the clinic first before we let them in. People could not enter the clinic unless they had an appointment, and they had to answer the questionnaire on the phone if they had lived with someone positive for COVID-19 or were at potential risk of getting in contact with someone positive with COVID-19 and if they had any COVID-19 symptoms. Once inside the clinic, we would check their temperature to see if they have high fever. Patients who have had one or two COVID-19 symptoms must stay at home.

"This is why we came here at the clinic—because we are sick!" I heard one patient say to the front desk receptionist.

I went back to help Melanie with the papers.

When I finished helping Melanie, she thanked me for helping her. I sanitized the waiting area again. It was a show-off because I wanted them to see I was working hard and following the clinic's protocols. I went for an hour break, but it was supposed to be half an hour; the clinic staff were friendly and would give students an hour break time.

When I finished my break, I went to the front desk counter and looked for a thermometer behind it when I heard them talking about a patient with COVID-19 symptoms.

"He sneezed as he left through the door." One of the front desk staff said.

"Ask the student to clean the doors," Melanie said.

"Did he have covid?" The nurse asked.

"Maybe, but he had a runny nose and sneezing a lot." The desk representative said.

I overheard them talking as I took the body temperature from the front desk. Then the nurse saw me.

"Rainna, can you sanitize the doors and all the chairs." The nurse said.

"Yeah, for sure," I answered, sanitizing the door handles and chairs.

I felt so low about myself as a student. *'Why are they making me do the dirty work?'* I thought. They wanted me to sanitize the doors because someone who probably had COVID-19 sneezed as he walked through them.

I washed my hands thoroughly. Every hand-washing sink had instructions posted, mainly beside the hand soap or the paper hand towel dispenser. We had to wash our hands for twenty seconds, dry our hands first with a paper towel, and turn the faucet off with the used paper towel. We shouldn't touch the faucet with our bare, clean hands because it has been considered dirty since we first held it with dirty hands.

We had to sanitize the chairs each time a patient sat on them, and the chairs were 6 feet apart. I learned more in my placement than in school, and I felt embarrassed that I didn't know some things I should have known.

Two weeks before my placement was almost done, I knew I wanted to work at the clinic, but I also knew they wouldn't hire me. Although it wasn't wrong to hope for the best.

Melanie spent 20 minutes giving me feedback on the papers to show to my college admins and was proud that I finished my placement. She gave me the papers and said, "I will keep you in mind."

After my college placement and on my way to work, I searched for jobs on Indeed to see if front desk receptionists were hiring in my area. I found a couple of them, and on my break at the fast food job, I sent a bunch of resumes to the hiring clinics near me. A few weeks after my college placement, I never got any calls from any of the clinics I applied for.

43

FAILED EXAM

After finishing my college placement, I asked Antonio if I could work only once a week for three weeks until my scheduled certification exam. He allowed me to work only once a week for three weeks.

"If you ever fail the exam, you can apply as a supervisor," he said jokingly, and we laughed.

'No, thanks.' I thought. I laughed with Antonio. I was hoping that the jobs I applied for would call me sooner and would quit fast food at any time soon.

I only had three weeks to study everything that I didn't learn from online school. I hated myself for not having self-discipline in studying, and instead of revising my notes, it was my first time learning the materials, but I studied diligently and hoped to pass the exam. I like learning, but I wouldn't say I enjoyed studying for the exam. That made me anxious. I could not focus on studying because my dying cat jumped onto my lap, and I couldn't avoid my cat but cuddled with her. I wanted to spend more time with her since I knew she wouldn't be here long.

Bruno ghosted me again for maybe the nth time. I was scared, paranoid, and having an anxiety attack. I had so many excuses for not studying, but I tried my best to study every day. I bought the needed books and took some practice exams, but I was distracted by social media. I took pictures of myself studying for the exam, posted them, and waited for

Bruno to view my Instagram story. But he never did, and waiting for him to message me was a wasted time.

Whenever I worked on Saturday, I would stay in bed for a few hours because even though I only worked once a week, my body was tired and could not move. I would bring my notes to work, but I mostly didn't end up studying because the store was loud. The machines at work were beeping. The kitchen staff yelled because they needed a product in the front. One of the supervisors sounded like she was panicking because they thought we didn't have gravy, but one kitchen staff made extra gravy.

"Make more gravy!" The supervisor said.

'Can't say please?' I thought.

I could hear the people who bred the chickens goofing around, and I heard something fall. It might have been the big pot or perhaps a co-worker who fell. They were all laughing, and Rolland went to the back and yelled at them. I couldn't understand what Rolland was saying, but he was mad.

'I don't think I can study.' I thought.

I went to the front to get something to eat. Since I would rather not study at work than starve, Rolland put my order on the cash register and made the food for me.

Two days before my scheduled exam, I remembered that I could have been studying for months instead of waiting for Bruno to love me back. I remembered my brother's friend, a nurse, saying, "One day before the exam, you should be resting." But in my case, I had to stay up late to study everything because I didn't finish my study materials.

On the day of my exam, I knew I would fail. The questions were tricky, but I knew I hadn't studied enough. I stared at my computer blankly.

We had three hours to take the exam, and we would know the results right after we pressed the submit button.

Once I hit submit, I read the words "did not pass," and my heart sank.

My classmate texted me and asked me if I had passed, and I said, "No."

She said, "Same. I threw up when I got the result."

I knew I would fail, but I never knew I would be more frustrated seeing the exam result. I knew I wouldn't pass, yet I still hoped to pass the exam. I felt like the world hated me. I felt like a failure, dumb, unsuccessful. I was afraid I might be stuck in a fast-food job forever and would have to accept the supervisory position my manager offered me twice.

'I should not be embarrassed and feel shame. You did that to yourself. It would be best if you had been studying instead of flirting with boys,' I told myself.

I took a 50-minute shower, and a train of thought occupied my mind. I repeatedly told myself that I was a failure.

'You did that to yourself. Why are you sad? You're not allowed to be.'

'You're dumb. What's new? You barely pass 1st grade. You almost failed grade 1 because you didn't know how to read and do basic math.'

'It's okay. Just take the supervisor position. You'd be good at it.'

'No one would hire you in the medical field.'

'Why would I hope for more incredible things in life? I am a failure. I failed the exam.'

My thoughts hurt me because it was the truth. I barely passed first grade. I didn't want to stay at fast food because I knew it wouldn't be enough. I couldn't imagine myself working for years as a minimum wage earner where I could find a better job that pays well.

I told my mom about it, and she said, "It's okay. Maybe it's not time yet. How many times can you take it?"

"Three times. I failed the first try, so I still have two more tries." I said while we were eating on the couch.

I didn't check my phone, but I felt compelled to message one of my friends already working as a Medical Lab Technician.

She said, "We are hiring. Just send your resume using this link."

I sent my resume using the link she sent me, hoping that I would get a chance to get a job in the medical field. I cuddled with my cat, fed her food, and gave her treats. Treat foods are like chocolates for them, and she loved it.

That night, Bruno texted me. "Hey beautiful, how are you."

My heart jumped for joy. I could not believe that Bruno had messaged me; yes, he became my happiness. I could not let him go and would forgive him every time he stopped texting me.

"Hey, handsome. I'm not okay. How have you been?" I replied.

"Why aren't you okay?" He asked.

"I failed the certification exam but can still retake it," I said.

"That's okay. Don't worry about it. Why don't you take a flight to Yellowknife?" He said.

"Why? Are you in Yellowknife?" I asked.

"Yeah. They moved me here." He said.

He sent me a black-and-white picture of himself in a white shirt and cargo pants. It was a mirror selfie with his back.

"I was bulking and shaved my head. I am bald now." He said.

"That's nice. And how long have you been staying there? Aren't you coming to Sauga for Christmas?" I said.

"No"

"Oh, why not? Come back here! I miss you!" I said.

"I'll come back for you. Rent a hotel for a week, just you and me. We can sleep all day long. Forget about your exams, and be away from everybody." He said.

My heart melted from his words.

"Yeah, sure. I loved that!." I said.

But deep inside, I knew something was wrong. It was great that he wanted to spend time with me, but I felt my body didn't accept what Bruno said.

We still talked for two days, then he disappeared again. However, I forgot about the failed exams. Bruno was a great distraction for me. I would lay a path for him and cross the ocean. I didn't go to Yellowknife to see him, although I wanted to. I didn't know where I would be staying, and I didn't know what excuse I would be telling my family to go to Yellowknife. I couldn't tell my family that I was meeting somebody in Yellowknife. It would be a great shame for me that I failed the exam, yet I was going to meet somebody.

Part

V

NTH TIME WAVE 2022

44

HEAVY SNOW

I had an opening morning shift during a heavy snowstorm. I was scheduled for work at 07:00 and had to take an Uber because I would be late if I chose to ride the bus. When I called for the Uber, I was shocked by the price. On that hectic day, the Uber cost me $80 Canadian dollars. to travel about 8.5 kilometres from my place, while the regular Uber price was about $15 Canadian dollars. Since it was snowing heavily and booking an Uber ride was also in demand, the fare was at a surcharge rate.

While waiting for my Uber ride, I posted a story on my Instagram with a screenshot of how much my Uber cost.

I said, "This is injustice."

One of my co-workers who was supposed to be working with me that day replied to my Instagram story and said,

"Girl, you should have called in sick like I did. I called in; there was no way I would be paying that much.".

Then Lester said, "You worked a lot of hours, only to fund your one way ride to the fast food for one morning."

I barely called in sick at work because I knew that I needed to work and had bills to pay, and calling in sick was not in my mind. All I knew was I needed to get there to set up the store and prepare for opening shifts.

"I think we are not going to open today since many team members called in sick, and we may not have customers today," said Jeyja in a text message.

'It can't be. No. The store could not close for that day since they didn't announce it earlier.' I thought.

When the Uber driver arrived after I had waited for 25 minutes, he didn't pick me up from my exact location. I had to walk towards the outer area of my street to get in his car since the Uber driver could not drive through the snow on my street. The snow was below my knees, and I was about 5 feet tall as a short girl. The Uber car smelled terrible, and his car was hot. I was wearing my uniform, a sweater, winter hat, disposable mask, and a winter jacket. The Uber driver had a winter jacket, a winter hat, and a mask below his chin. It annoyed me to see people with masks below their chin because why would they wear their masks if they wouldn't wear them properly?

Uber drivers had a hard time driving through the road, and they had to drive slowly. It was 6:47 in the morning, and there was no way that I would get there by 7:00 on time. I texted Jeyja and told her that I would be late. Then, Antonio texted me and asked where I was, and I said,

"I'm on my way to the store."

"We may not open today because of the bad snowstorm," Antonio replied.

I was 6 kilometres from my place, and the Uber driver had difficulty driving through heavy snow. I had to pay $80 Canadian dollars for my Uber ride, and the management would tell me that we would not open today because there wouldn't be any customers since it was snowing.

'How great, isn't it?' I thought sarcastically.

I felt intense sweat on my hands. I stared blankly through the car window, watching other people plow the snow so their cars could pass. I barely saw people walking on the snow-covered sidewalks. It was heavily snowing, and it was hard to navigate the road. Some cars were stuck on the side road, and I saw the bus and its trunk were open, perhaps due to damage or malfunction.

'Why didn't the management tell us earlier? The news said the night before that there would be a snowstorm.' I thought.

The Uber driver managed to drive near the store and said, "Miss, this is the way only I can drive you. You walk there."

I was in a lousy mood to fight the Uber driver for not dropping me off at my destination. The Uber driver struggled with English and mumbled some words I couldn't understand. Then, he called customer service, putting him on hold for ten minutes. I argued that I paid $80 Canadian dollars for the ride, and he didn't want to drop me at my destination. He then handed me his phone when a representative of Uber was ready to speak, and the Uber driver said, "Tell them," "What do you want me to say?" I asked him back.

I didn't ask him to call a customer support service; I needed him to drop me off at my location. We were on the other street, and he wanted me to walk to my destination.

"Hi, I have a passenger, and it's snowing; I can't drive there," he complained to Uber customer service.

Hearing that from the driver pissed me off.

"Excuse me, it's the Uber's passenger. Listen, I paid 80 bucks for my ride, but the Uber driver didn't want to drive to my destination!" I said angrily.

The Uber driver scratched his right ear. Then, he told customer service about refunding me.

"I am not going to leave your car unless you drop me off at my destination. Look how far we are from my destination! This is not 80 dollars, sir." I shook my head no. I removed my seat belt and opened the car window.

"Close the window," he demanded.

I was having a bad morning. I had spent 80 Canadian dollars on an Uber ride, only to be told we weren't opening in a heavy snowstorm. I didn't want to close the car window; the interior car smelled terrible despite wearing a disposable mask, and I needed to breathe. I was shaking in anger and breathing heavily.

"I will not close it until you drop me to my destination," I sternly warned him.

"Miss, I can't drive there. There's heavy snow, too much," he insists.

I knew a car would blow up if forced to drive through heavy snow, but I requested a deal with him despite that.

"If you can't drop me off at my exact destination, could you please drive me a little bit closer? I will also refund this. This is awful," I said.

He drove me a little closer. I walked through heavy snow below the knee-deep. I heard the wind hissing and crunching my footsteps on fresh snow.

I felt terrible for complaining and raising my voice to the Uber driver, but I was in a bad mood. It's almost becoming a bad day. I complained that the Uber driver didn't pick me up from my pick-up location and didn't drop me off at my exact destination, and I had to pay $80 Canadian dollars to get to work that we wouldn't be opening.

'Will Fast Food pay for my Uber?' I thought to myself.

I was having a hard time walking through the snow. I could barely see the road. A few bunches of snow stacked up on places that looked like mountains. There were a few cars covered with snow. I saw a guy cleaning off the sidewalk in front of our store.

I called Antonio to find out if we were opening that day and to ensure that my effort of coming despite the snowstorm would not be wasted. I said, "Hello, Antonio, are we still opening today? I'm already here outside the store."

"You can open the door." Said Antonio.

He gave me the password and the code for the store to open. Usually, it was the supervisor's job to open the store, but Antonio had given me and trusted me to open it myself.

"I am going there with Jeyja. We still have to clean the driveway, okay? We'll open the store when we get there, but do the prep," said he.

Jeyja and Antonio lived closer together, and they were on their way.

Antonio instructed me to open the store and prepare for the opening shift. By 9:30, I entered the store, placed my bag in the locker in the break room and opened the kitchen station machines. I played some music to set the mood despite the crippling cold wind blowing outside, and I posted a story on my Instagram about me going to work through a heavy snowstorm.

While waiting for the kitchen machines to heat up, I went to the dining room to see what the parking lot looked like through the window glass. Then I heard a bang in the kitchen. I ran up and saw a pile of snow fall from the roof. I grabbed my phone in the breakroom and took a video of it. I sent the video to Antonio.

"Oh no! We need to fix it! Uhm, Uhm, clean it, and we'll figure that out later. We are still here; we'll be there maybe in thirty minutes." Antonio replied.

I felt him panicking about the snowfall in our kitchen. It was a huge mess, but I could clean it up.

When I checked the situation outside, there were no people on site. It was snowing heavily. I felt terrible for the Uber driver again, but I was stressed out because they charged me more than it should have cost. I checked my credit card online and saw that Uber had charged me $125.00 Canadian dollars. It got under my skin, gave me goosebumps, and hardened my heart.

'That was a huge amount!' I thought.

By 11:30, Jeyja and Antonio arrived, and then we opened the store for customers. People ordered through online delivery, but very few delivery drivers were available. Some customers called to place the order, and a few customers came in.

Antonio approached me and said, "Send me the receipt of your Uber, and Fast Food will pay for it, okay?"

'Fast Food will pay for my overly expensive Uber ride today? What a huge relief?!' I thought. I thought to myself while worrying about the fare I had paid earlier. The stress I'd been carrying regarding my Uber ride this morning was relieved.

One of my co-workers, Edward, came in late and fried the chicken, and then Adrianna arrived. We didn't have many customers, and we planned to close early. Antonio had let Edward, Jeyja, and I get soup noodles from the next-door market.

"Yeah, free food! Haha!" I said as I enthusiastically grabbed the food.

"Did you guys drive from Oakville to here in Sauga?" I asked Jeyja.

"No, we took an Uber, too! Hahaha," Jeyja said.

"Yeah, I didn't wanna drive with heavy snow on the road." Antonio said.

Some customers came in with big orders, but the store wasn't busy that day due to snowstorms. By 6:30 in the evening, we had prepared to close and cleaned up.

"You are a hard worker, Rainna, a true employee of Fast Food." Adrianna complimented me.

"Thank you for coming, Rainna," Antonio said.

It was the first time I heard Antonio appreciate me. I haven't heard him say, 'Thank you' for the last two years of working with him in the store; his gratitude that day was a total surprise.

"Don't forget to get a refund. They charged you way too much!" Adrianna said.

"Yep, I won't," I replied.

We all locked the doors and took an Uber to go home. Addrianna's husband came to pick her up. I had taken an Uber, and so did Jeyja and Antonio.

Because of the heavy snow, I opened and closed the store for two days in a row.

45

"REMIND YOUR STAFF TO SMILE."

I worked with Jeyja and Chris on a typical Monday morning. Jeyja was doing a supervisory duty in the office, Chris was preparing the chicken, and I was preparing the front counter before we opened the store for the customers. We changed our opening time to eight o'clock in the morning until eight o'clock in the evening. I turned on the menu board and the fountain drinks. I asked Chris to help me arrange the chairs in the dine-in area since we opened the dine-in area for the customers, but there were still precautions to take. The plexiglass was installed on each of the dine-in chairs for social distancing.

We were handling some important tasks when one of our colleagues who was supposed to be working at the front called in sick, leaving us shorthanded.

"Guys!!! Fatima called in sick!" Jeyja said.

"Uh-oh, Rainna's gonna work on the front. Haha," Chris said.

"No way! When's the next person coming?" I asked Jeyja.

"Ten o'clock," Jeyja said, looking at the schedule.

"Tsk! I have to work for two freaking hours in the front! Is it okay to ask the next person to come in early?" I asked Jeyja, annoyed.

Unfortunately, the next person to arrive wasn't scheduled until 10:00. As we continued to work, I suddenly felt some discomfort in my stomach. It was a sharp, twisting pain that was hard to ignore. I suspected what it could be since I had consumed coffee on an empty stomach. Although I'm aware that this is not a healthy habit, I tend to do it quite often. I wasn't feeling good that day and felt like I needed to go home. Despite the discomfort, I tried my best to push through and continue working alongside my team. However, the pain persisted and made it difficult for me to focus. Jeyja put me in the front for a while. She would do my job in the kitchen, and Chris would cook the chicken and make fries.

As of April 2022, we were still wearing masks, which was mandatory.

It was a beautiful day outside, with the sun shining brightly and a cool breeze blowing. Fifteen minutes before we opened the store for customers, I noticed three people waiting outside our store. I didn't feel like taking any customer orders at that moment because, from the looks of it, it would be a busy day. I knew many people would be out and about, taking advantage of the gorgeous weather to enjoy the day.

I wished I could join the people outside and enjoy the lovely weather instead of being uncomfortable at work. The sun's rays glared through the glass window, sometimes making it hard to see.

"Can we open at least two minutes late? Haha, I don't feel like taking orders." I laughed after asking Jeyja.

I told Jeyja jokingly, but I meant it 90% truthfully. Jeyja didn't like what I said; she ignored me and went to the office.

At precisely eight o'clock, Jeyja opened the entrance door. I stood at the cash register, and I was not ready to take the orders of the early morning customers.

"Hi there, good morning. Welcome to Fast Food; what can I get for you?" I said to the customer.

Then the customer asked, "Do you guys have breakfast? Like an egg sandwich or something with eggs?"

"We don't carry breakfast." I shook my head no.

"Oh, okay. What do you guys have?" she asked, and she removed her mask.

'Was she trying to provoke me? Did she not see the big screen menu over my head?' I thought.

As soon as the woman's words left her mouth, a strong and sudden emotion of annoyance swept through me. It was as if a wave had washed over me, making me agitated. I couldn't believe what she had said. I tried to make sense of her statement without taking my eyes off her.

I stared at her intensely, trying to read her expression. My mind was racing with questions and doubts, but I didn't let it show. I maintained my composure and continued to observe her quietly. Our menu boards were big and clear enough for her to see 15 feet away from the counter. I read the menu for her just in case she didn't like the giant menu board.

"We have chicken, burgers, fries, and some drinks. You can check on your side," said I.

Then she said, "I can't hear you."

Everyone at work was struggling to communicate with each other. We barely heard anyone talk clearly since our voices were muffled by the masks we were wearing. I took a deep breath and looked at her.

I pointed to the menu board and said, "These are what we have."

The lady took about two minutes to decide, while three more customers entered our restaurant. I wanted to tell the customer to wear her mask, but at that point, I just wanted to go with the flow and work on autopilot.

"Oh my gosh, a lot of people are here early," Jeyja said.

Jeyja quickly took the next customer's order and helped me take theirs. She efficiently took the next customer's order, and I couldn't help but notice how swiftly she did it. However, the lady I was attending to was still on the phone, conversing with someone on the other end for a good ten minutes. It seemed as though she was taking orders from a group of people. I couldn't help but feel a little impatient, but I reminded myself to be kind and courteous, just like Jeyja.

The lady finally ordered ten burgers, not a combo. I asked her if she wanted them with cheese.

She said, "Just the way it is, no pickles and no tomatoes."

Then I said, "We don't put pickles and tomatoes on our burger. But we put cheese on..."

I wasn't finished talking when she cut me off and said loudly, "Just no cheese."

"Okay. Do you wanna make them a combo with sides and drinks?" I asked.

She answered, "No."

I had a gut feeling that the lady might be interested in ordering a meal combo. To confirm and avoid confusion, I repeated my question to her, saying,

"Sorry, just to confirm, you don't want any drinks with your burgers, right?"

This was evident when I took her orders. I ensured that what I put on the cash register was correct.

"Yes." She answered,

She positioned her card in the card transaction.

"Will that be all for today?" I asked her for the last confirmation.

"Yes." Said she.

I admit I was not happy. I was polite, but I gave the customer a dirty look. I was uncomfortable taking orders while I was in pain. I felt like I needed to sit down, but the customer took a lot of time to order, and she gave me an attitude by raising her voice at me.

She paid for her order, and I gave her the receipt.

"It's gonna take ten minutes for your order," I politely told the customer.

She looked at the receipt and didn't say anything, then put back her mask on. I took the next two customers quickly; they all had small orders.

Jeyja assembled their orders, and I helped her with drink orders. The lady waited for less than ten minutes since Jeyja quickly made her order.

Then, Jeyja said, "Here you go, ten burgers, no cheese," as she handed the lady a bag of burgers.

Then the lady asked, "Where's the drink?"

Jeyja and I looked at each other, and I said,

"She didn't order it."

"Do you want a combo or just drinks?" Jeyja asked the customer.

"Combo." The lady said.

I went to the breakroom, and Chris was there drinking water.

Then I said to Chris, "What the f*ck? That m*ther f*cking customer doesn't know how to f*cking order. Stupid arse."

Chris laughed. "Just calm down."

"Where are you guys at? Come to the front." Jeyja said.

I wanted to sit down, but I couldn't. I tried to hide in the office room to avoid the customer, and I didn't want to see the lady because my blood was boiling for her. If I hadn't avoided her, I might have said something wrong to her. Telling Jeyja that she wanted a combo after her order and that the transaction was done was disrespectful.

I noticed that some customers would claim they didn't want a combo meal, but after receiving their order, they would lie and say they had ordered a combo to receive free items. They would order specific items and then claim their order was incorrect, asking if they could also take the "mistake" order. Jeyja was punching orders and making them combos.

The customer said, "That's… that's the price?"

The lady was shocked by the total cost of her order. I went to the kitchen to make more burger patties while Chris made some fries. I could hear their conversation from the front.

"Yes, ten burger combos with fries and drinks," Jeyja said.

"Okay. That's it." The customer said.

I went back to talk to Chris and said,

"That customer is confused. Just like my man. Haha! My man can't decide whether he loves me or not. Haha!"

That was the kind of joke I would say and a kind of joke that Chris and I would understand.

"You got a man? Haha! Is your bebe the customer? Haha!" said Chris.

I laughed to ease my anger and returned to the front, where I prepared the drinks for the lady. Ten drinks later, we were almost out of the drink trays.

I rolled my eyes at the customer, but she didn't see me rolling my eyes. She was looking at the receipt. At the bottom of our receipt is a website where customers can leave feedback.

'She definitely would leave us feedback.' I thought.

An hour later, when we had downtime, Jeyja went to the office and did some supervisor stuff, and we received feedback from the lady. We couldn't see the names or emails of the people who gave us feedback, but we all knew that lady was the one who gave us input because we didn't give the other customers the receipt. Some customers left their receipts on the counter and the table where they had dined. The lady gave us a good review on the food and left a comment saying,

"Tell your staff to smile; they are front liners."

'Yes, that's me. She is talking about me,' I thought. I had no defence because I was caught in the act.

Then I said, "I was 'the staff' and needed to be reminded to smile."

"Who's going to smile when you are that kind of customer? How did you know we weren't smiling? We're wearing masks." I said, talking to the screen. "Like, she gave me an unpleasant attitude and expected me to smile at her? The heck is she thinking?"

"Yeah, just leave it," Jeyja said.

"Who are you to tell us to smile? Hahaha!" I said sarcastically.

"Rainna needs her bebe. Hahaha! Don't worry, he's going to come later." Chris said.

We burst into laughter. That was how we coped with stress and negativity. I left the office and went to the break room, where I finally sat for my ten-minute break. While sitting on a chair, Benny came in early.

"You can go back to your kitchen station since Benny is here," Jeyja said.

"Okay," I said.

I never felt bad for getting a bad review, but somehow, I felt guilty. The customer gave me an attitude, and I tried to be as polite as possible despite my uncomfortable situation.

'I'm a human being too, and I have feelings.' I thought.

I stared blankly at the wall in the break room while waiting for my short break to finish, and I wondered if a customer would be so lovely, would the fast-food worker be rude to the customers? I never thought so. I had given the customer an attitude because I made sure she didn't want a combo, yet she insisted that she didn't want combos, and when she got her order, she asked for combos. When we again punched in her order as combos, she was shocked about the price of the food item. She also cut me off while I was still talking.

'Like, I'm sorry, I already had a bad day, and meeting a customer like her ruined my day shift.' I thought.

46

DOWNTIME

"I remember when the pandemic was new, I didn't wanna wear a mask," I told Chris.

"Same! It was hard to breathe. Now, I can't leave the house without it." Chris said.

"Right. It's like, it's part of the outfit now." I said.

Chris and I talked a lot about work while we were working. He was frying the chicken, and while waiting for the chicken to finish, he made some fries ready for the opening shift.

"Don't make too many fries," Jeyja said.

"Okay," Chris said.

During our downtime, Chris and I would discuss the memes and funny videos we've watched on social media.

"I love quiet time like this," I said.

"So peaceful," Chris said.

"Later on, we'll hear the customers complaining for nothing, saying we don't smile, HAHAHHA," I said laughingly.

"You're gonna see your bebe later," Chris said, teasing me.

I laughed at him. Chris teased me about the customer who comes in daily for a burger combo. Every time that man came in, Chris would say he was my boyfriend. I went to the back to wash some dishes. I heard some beeping machine noise, and the ice cubes fell heavily into the ice cube machine. The floors were slippery, while cleaning the scoop for the soup. Suddenly, a big pot fell on my head. I wasn't sure if I should react or ignore the fact that a big pot had dropped on me.

'*The management wouldn't care about it anyway,*' I thought.

I was shocked and went to Jeyja in the office and said,

"The pot fell on me," pressing my head with both hands while telling me what had happened to me.

Jeyja asked, "Are you okay?"

I said, "Yeah, but it kinda hurts."

She said, "Put some ice on it".

"Oh, that's the boink sound I heard," Chris said.

I laughed at him; it was hilarious that he heard the bang in the back of the kitchen. I placed ice cubes in a small plastic bag on my head to ease the pain and drank a lot of water. While working, I put the small bag filled with ice cubes on my head for an hour. I used my other hand to hold the plastic bag filled with ice and the other hand to prepare food. Sometimes, I would use both hands and balance my head while the plastic bag with ice was on my head; it was a good thing it didn't fall.

"I hope you're okay," Chris said.

"HAHAHA! It's okay; I fell harder for him." I said jokingly.

"Ayee! HAHAHA! Is that your bebe?" Chris said.

In Filipino culture, "*hugot*" means to "pull out" in English. It means pulling something deep within our emotions' roots and expressing them through wisecracks.

"*Hugot*" is usually sentimental, one short sentence about heartache or romantic love. Chris and I would share some "*hugot*" when we were bored. Chris would always make cheesy comments about Jena. I didn't have a boyfriend or someone I was talking to romantically. Besides, I was losing hope with Bruno. Painful and heart-aching "*hugot*" was always for me. We joked about my imaginary boyfriend and the customer who always comes in the morning, and they tried to link me with the customer in a romantic but joking manner.

In my previous fast-food job, we had to record every accident, such as what happened to me, pots falling on our heads, minor cuts on our fingers, and burns. However, the fast-food restaurant where I worked during the COVID-19 pandemic didn't care much about team members' safety.

'This fast-food restaurant is not for beginners,' I thought.

Two weeks later, when I was washing the scoop needed for mashed potatoes, the same big pot fell on me and hit harder this time.

"Ouch!!!" I screamed and dropped the scoop to the sink.

"Aahhhhh!! It hurts!" I ran to the break room and pressed my head hard with my hands.

"What happened?" Chris walked to the breakroom and asked,

"The pot fell on my head again! Ouch! It hurts!" I replied.

"How many times does the pot need to fall on you for you to realize that he couldn't love you?" Chris asked jokingly.

"The pot fell on my head many times, and I still can't fathom how much it hurts to love him. Hahaha! *Hugot*! Eeww! cringe!" I sarcastically said.

Chris laughed. I laughed in pain.

"I wish someone would fall in love with me the way the big pot fell on my head! HAHAHAHA! *Hugot* again!" I blurted the joke, and we all laughed.

I again placed the ice cubes in a small plastic bag, ensuring they were secure. Then, I gently positioned the bag on my head, using the same way I had used the last time the pot fell on me.

"I think I'm getting used to it now, eh?" I said to Chris.

"Yeah! You're getting used to getting hurt." Chris said, trying to make me cry for being a hopeless romantic.

"Ouch! That hurts! Hahaha." I joked.

47

BE PATIENT

It is cliche to say, "Be patient," but it is one of the hardest things to learn. I lose myself occasionally and sometimes can't control my emotions. However, working at a fast-food restaurant during the pandemic taught me patience.

While working at a fast-food restaurant, wearing a mask and face shield, it was hard for me to communicate and talk to people properly since my voice was naturally soft and low. I had to speak louder, which was hard for me. It annoys me when a customer asks me to speak more audible, and it annoys me more when they ask me to repeat what I said.

When I asked a middle-aged lady if she wanted fries or mashed potatoes for her side, she couldn't even get what I was asking about.

"You can get mashed potatoes or fries for the sides," I said.

"Sooo, for the combo? What is that?" The customer said.

"For combo, you will get a side and a drink of your choice," I said.

"What? I can't hear you." She said.

I explained what comes with our burger combo, and she couldn't get it for the last five minutes. Then, she said, "Okay, the uhmmm, the uhm, what's that again? The mashed potato." she said.

"You want the mashed potatoes for your sides?" I asked her for confirmation.

"Yes. hmmm." She answered.

She wanted mashed potatoes for her side. I cashed her into our cash register. We took her orders and gave the food orders to her within five minutes. It was a slow day; few people were in the line. I wiped the counters and a few trays, changed my gloves, and washed my hands.

"Good job, Rainna, for washing your hands. Look at Rainna washing her hands." Antonio said.

I laughed because I didn't know what to say. I wasn't sure if Antonio was being sarcastic or serious about applauding me for washing my hands, but it was necessary to wash our hands often.

About 15 minutes later, the middle-aged lady came back and screamed at me in broken English,

"Where is my fries? I order combo! You.. you not listening to me. I want for combo and there no fries!"

She looked upset because she didn't have fries for her order.

"Ma'am, you ordered a combo with mashed potatoes for your side, not fries," I said.

I explained to her with my gasping breath that our combo comes with fries or mashed potatoes, and since she chose mashed potatoes as her combo's side, she'll receive mashed potatoes.

'What is going on with your small mind, woman?' I thought.

I couldn't understand what was happening in customer's heads when ordering. I accommodated them as much as possible and explained how our combos work and what comes as their drinks and sides.

'Keep your cool, Rainna, it's just another dumb customer. You'll be okay,' I thought.

"Okay, I will give you the fries," I said.

I took the mashed potatoes from the customer's plastic bag and gave her fries. I threw the mashed potatoes to the trashcan and the customer left.

"Is it okay if I go on my break now?" I asked Jeyja.

"Yes, you can, while there's no customer," Jeyja said.

I thought I was losing my patience with the customer, but I have yet to learn patience. I went on my break and scrolled through my Facebook account. Most of my Facebook friends were Christians. Since I started Facebook during my early teens, I added a lot of people from the church I was attending in the Philippines. Then, one of my Facebook friends posted a Bible quote that said, *"Rejoice in our confident hope. Be patient in trouble, and keep on praying.—Romans 12:12"*.

'Wow! This is timely.' I thought.

I repeated the Bible verse in my head to be patient. Then, I realized that moment when a customer screamed at me; it wasn't me who showed the wrong side but the customer. I understood why people were upset, but imperfect people also operate fast-food restaurants. We tried our best and sometimes made mistakes, too, but we can never be wrong for being patient. At the end of the day, we still had our lives together; we still showed up for our work duty, and we didn't lose anything. Screaming and frustrated customers would come to pass.

When I returned to the front of our store, Antonio sent me to take orders at the entrance door.

"Maintain social distancing, and remember the mask policy," Antonio said, and I nodded.

I took the tablet we used to take orders outside and began taking orders. I took an order at the entrance, and we had a six-foot-apart policy. These two ladies, who were together, kept moving closer to me as they ordered, and I kept moving backward away from them. Antonio saw it, talked to me through the headset, and reminded me about being six feet apart.

"Can both of you move backwards? You're getting close to me," I told the ladies.

They had big orders, costing them about $300 Canadian dollars. We had to split the order since our cash register couldn't accept large amounts of money. I had to repeat the order to double-check it with them, and as I was repeating the order, they were talking to each other and were not listening to me. I got annoyed. I felt intense on my forehead. I was giving them a dirty look and rolling my eyes. They noticed how pissed I was, and they still gave me a hard time. They ordered more food from us and kept closer to me. I had to remind them again to back off.

"Rainna, how long will it take for that order to finish? They're holding the line." Antonio asked me through the headset.

Our headsets were among the most essential tools for communicating. I ignored Antonio because my blood started to boil, and I felt hot.

'Well, it was not my fault that the customer had big orders,' I thought.

Chase helped me take orders; he had another tablet with him. After taking the two ladies' orders, I took the next twenty customers with big orders.

"Oh my gosh, it is so busy!" I said to Chase.

"I know girl, but we got this!" Chase said, assuring that we can get through the busy day.

Two hours later, I went inside and told Antonio I needed to take my thirty-minute break. Antonio also sent Chase on the break, which made me happy since Chase would take a break with me. I had to take three deep breaths in the breakroom without wearing a mask.

"I've had enough with customers," I said to Chase, who was eating in the breakroom.

"Aw, it's okay," said Chase, patting my shoulder.

"I didn't like the two ladies; they pissed me off," I said. "Like, I told them more than twice to move backwards 'cause they're getting close to me."

Chase hugged me for comfort. I had to remind myself to be patient during hard times because if not, I'd only suffer from getting annoyed by people.

'Be patient and kind and let it go.' I thought.

"Just relax," said Chase.

I learned that patience helps me remain calm under pressure. Some customers didn't have patience in waiting, but it would be an outrage if I didn't have patience as a worker. I didn't want to lose my job because I lost my patience while taking orders. Since then, I have always tried to remember to be patient in times of trouble. I knew my faith was at a low point at that time. I cursed a lot, and it was hard for me to return to the Lord.

Time sped up, and the store was closing; I rushed home. I couldn't wait to be home, be authentic, and write my thoughts down.

That night, I wrote in my journal:

"Sometimes, I notice when there is something wrong with me. Seeing how my co-workers worked, I saw that they were perfectly fine. But I have had enough. Perhaps they are younger and full of life than I am. They didn't think about the job, but maybe they enjoyed their work. But

I have had enough. I may have been old enough to work at a fast-food restaurant. But it was all I had. I didn't know any other suitable job, and as someone who only graduated from high school, I knew nobody would ever hire me. Nobody would ever bother calling me for an interview."

During a busy work day, nonstop working and taking orders in person and online, everything that happened during the day played in my head like a film. The sound of an online order being placed, and we had to accept it, the advance call for big food orders, and the people giving us a hard time. Every detail of what had happened in a day played in my mind as if it was a bad short movie you couldn't forget.

I knew that I was never a patient person, but it reminded me of Bruno's calm and collected nature. Despite all that happened, I wanted to learn to be patient and calm like Bruno. I tried to stay calm because I wouldn't want to work when my heart beat fast or annoyed.

"Rainna had anger issues," said my co-worker who got her ankle sprained; she looked at me with squinted eyes.

I never asked why she said that, but it all made sense. I had no patience, but I was learning and knew I was a work in progress.

48

LIFE OUTSIDE OF WORK

I waited for my bus ride when I finished my day's work. I could not stop thinking about the customers we encountered every day.

'When is this gonna end? I'm so tired of coming in for work every day. Wearing masks and gloves, taking customer's complaints,' I thought.

While waiting for the bus, I saw my co-worker, Charles, who was waiting, too. It was awkward to know a co-worker waiting for the same bus as me. There was plain silence and small talk, but I wished he wouldn't talk to me on the bus or sit beside me. Gladly, he felt uncomfortable; he didn't sit beside me during the bus ride. We both had earphones on, and he talked to his girlfriend, Kathy.

I'm not a fan of people getting into relationships from work, but Kathy and Charles met at a messy workplace, yet they were a perfect match.

They were stunningly beautiful and handsome. I was amazed by their story because Charles never wanted to date a Filipino until he met Kathy, and Kathy would like Asians but not Filipinos. Kathy and Charles were both Filipino, but Kathy was born and raised in Canada, and Charles was born in the Philippines and came to Canada as a kid. Kathy was bothered that Charles was a year younger than her, but Charles was mature enough to date Kathy.

I checked my social media account, and a delivery driver from work, Arnold, messaged me.

'How did this guy find me on social media?' I thought. *'I'll reply when I get home.'*

Whenever my work shift ends, I like to ride on the bus while listening to music without interruption. I was listening to "The Death Bed" song by Powfu non-stop while looking through the bus window. Streetlights glared through the bus window. I saw some old people who were walking with their masks on. Some were also riding a bicycle on the sidewalk with their mask on. The people on the bus were talking on the phone and speaking in their native language; some had a lot of grocery shopping bags, and the people seated on the bus went from five to fifteen people.

They were taking a few more passengers on the bus. Some bus drivers did not wear masks, but they had plexiglass between the side of their seats and the passengers, where we pay and tap our cards. I was expecting to see bus drivers wearing masks, yet it was weird that not all wear them during the pandemic.

When Charles got off the bus, he said goodbye to me, and I said, "See ya!".

When I got home, I opened Arnold's message.

"Hi, gorgeous," he said.

I felt uneasy since Bruno still held my heart, although I was already losing hope for Bruno, and I didn't want to entertain anyone but Bruno. I took a minute or so to reply to Arnold. Then I replied,

"Hey! Delivery for what name?" I said sarcastically since it was the question I always asked him at work when he was picking up food ordered for delivery.

"You are such a loser. How are you?" Said he.

"I'm good. Just finished work. Yourself?" I replied.

"Omg you worked today? Nothing, I decided to take a day off." Said he.

He then asked me if I was single and what happened to my last relationship. I told him that I was single and not looking for a relationship. I tried to reply as late as possible to let him know I was uninterested, but I admit I put him on the hook in case Bruno left me again. We continued chatting for about a week until he asked me if I wanted him to take a day off so we could go out.

"There are no coffee shops around us, lol, and I am busy every day," I said.

He ignored my last message, removed me from his followers and unfollowed me. Since then, I have never seen him at work to deliver food orders. I didn't mind Arnold leaving me since I was uninterested in him, and Bruno still had my heart.

I then realized that we had lives outside of work. We all felt what the customers felt. Just because we work at a fast-food restaurant and are considered "low-skill labourers" doesn't mean we are any less human. Our lives didn't revolve around taking orders and making food for customers. We, as fast food workers, fall in love, too. We got hurt. We got betrayed. In short, we have feelings, and we are humans too. We texted and called our loved ones during our break times and when we finished our shifts, no matter where they were. Some people forget that we are humans, too.

49

BETRAYAL

I dreaded myself to work. *'Urgh! Another day of working! Gotta wear freaken mask, face shield, and gloves while working!'* I thought. *'I'm so tired of everything!'*

One morning, I was called to the office because I had said something to our store manager, Antonio. I made terrible remarks about him because he didn't approve my time off request. Easter weekend 2022 was coming up. I requested the Easter weekend off a month in advance since I planned on staying at my brother and sister-in-law's house for the weekend. But Antonio still gave me a shift on that weekend. I was frustrated that he still gave me a work shift even though I had requested that weekend a month in advance.

Eventually, I told my brother that I couldn't come over for the Easter Weekend for a sleepover and to attend church. We both were frustrated because we were looking forward to spending time together as a family.

"It's alright," my brother replied.

My chin dipped to my chest, lips pressing tight. I held my tears and took a deep breath.

'I worked hard and barely called in sick. I did my job well and paid for my food on break. I would clock in and out on time for my starting, break, and ending shifts. I did what a good worker would and should do. Not getting

my time off request approved was something I took to heart because I didn't do anything wrong for them not to approve it.' I thought.

I texted Rebecca, saying that it pissed me off when Antonio posted a lot on social media about how we treat each other as a family and also about leadership. Still, how he was is the opposite of who he is in person. I was venting about how disappointed I was with my five closest co-workers in our work kitchen while preparing for the store before it opened for the day.

Antonio usually comes late. I needed to let my anger out of my chest because if I didn't, I would feel weak, break down and cry, but I thought strong people wouldn't cry. I wanted to be a person who never got hurt. Out of anger, I said terrible things about how bad of a manager he was.

I said, "Antonio didn't approve my request. F*ck him for not approving my time off request. I worked hard to request Easter weekend a month in advance and didn't receive what I requested. I knew they would need me on weekends, but I never got to take days off. Like, what the f*ck? What the f*ck, Antonio?"

I continued wiping off the counter, and every time I put something in the sink, I threw it hard. Four of my colleagues were doing their work while listening to me. Rebecca, Jeyja, Jena, and Jennica were there. Then I said,

"Didn't Antonio think they would need someone to cover me? I requested a month in advance. It's just so unfair. F*ck Antonio!"

As I walked back to the counter, stomping my feet, I exclaimed again, "F*ck Antonio!"

I noticed that my co-workers were silent. I knew I was safe with them because we all hang out outside work. We all swore terrible words, and there was no way they weren't comfortable with me swearing.

I continued venting out and said, "You would see him posting on social media saying 'we are family here' like the f*ck? Where is the family if you don't approve a request for time off for Easter?"

Two of our supervisors, Jena and Jeyja, were sweet until one of the supervisors who listened to my rant became bitter.

Two days later, I was called to the office regarding how I behaved and vented about our store manager, Antonio. I was called out for swearing, and he felt disrespected.

'How did Antonio know everything that I have vented? Someone must have told him. One of the five people I vented with must have told him.' I thought.

"I also heard that you complained about the rejected vacation request. It was called 'Request days off' because you cannot guarantee that it would be accepted. Nobody would be able to replace you." Antonio said calmly.

I wanted to burst into tears! I felt ashamed that I got caught! I was right, and somebody must have told Antonio about it. It was one of my four colleagues I vented out to. I knew my three other co-workers were against and hated him for different reasons. There was one person I realized later that should not be trusted.

I didn't answer Antonio's questions during the conversation with my supervisors. I let him talk for about 45 minutes. I thought to myself,

'Will that be my problem if they can't find someone to take my shift?'

But I also took that as a compliment and boosted my ego, saying they could not find someone to replace me.

"Was I that good at doing my job? Was I perfect that they couldn't find someone to replace me?' I thought.

When Antonio finished what he wanted to say, I said,

"I'm sorry for everything I said, and I promise I won't do it again." My throat was dry. Then, I left the office and worked my shift.

When I got home, I called Rebecca over the phone and told her about Antonio talking to me in the office. She immediately knew who it was. We both knew who had told Antonio about how I had vented.

I knew one of the supervisors I was close with told Antonio about it. She was the only one who could have done it because she was the manager's favourite pet. She was also the youngest supervisor, masked as a sheep but a goat behind the mask.

The next day, after they spoke to me, everyone was silent while we prepared the store to open at 8 a.m. I worked with Rebecca, Jeyja, and Chris that morning. Chris cracked a joke, and we all laughed except Jeyja, who pretended to be busy. I then started talking about one of the customers who would come in every day. Chris and I called that customer "Rainna's Bebe." We made fun of it because I was mostly single, and my co-workers were trying to find me a boyfriend. We talked while doing our duty, and Jeyja was quiet during the conversation.

I was wiping the tables in the dining area when Jeyja called me and said,

"You can start preparing your station in the kitchen."

She used to speak enthusiastically, but at that moment, she spoke slowly to me. Her voice was raspy and gravelly, reminiscent of rocks grinding together. Rebecca and I gave each other a side-eye. We both knew what was up. We both wanted to go to the break room to discuss Jeyja, but she would notice.

I felt something was up with Jeyja, but I didn't confront her. I sensed that she was feeling ashamed, but I ignored it. I wanted to continue working for another month before quitting. I remained quiet even though I was tempted to call her out that morning and ask why she told Antonio about what I said. I didn't want to retaliate and humiliate her because if I did, she was not going to like it, and it would make her cry. Her "Antonio" would fire me for making a scene. I didn't have that much power at work. I didn't have control over anyone at the Fast-food restaurant. I had to accept that life can be unfair at times.

I went to the kitchen to prepare my station. I had to make burger patties. Rebecca assembled parts on the soft drink machine, and Chris started breading the chicken. It was a sunny day, and I hoped for a better shift and not much of a customer complaint.

While waiting for the burger patty to be cooked, I contemplated asking Jeyja about what Antonio said, but I thought,

'What's the point? The damage has been done already.'

I decided to treat her in a civil way and not hold a grudge, even though I was curious about why she told Antonio. I am confused about letting go and letting things be with Jeyja or taking revenge. The battle within me was confusing, so I could not decide just yet. I was thinking about taking revenge by making her feel embarrassed for what she did or calling in sick at work. She had to cover for me when I called in sick for work as revenge, but I knew that taking revenge would only cause more problems.

Ultimately, I decided to be civil with her and treat her with respect. Besides, she was a supervisor and perhaps not a friend anymore. It was Jeyja who betrayed me and told Antonio everything that I had said. She has been one of my closest friends since we worked together, especially during the first wave of the pandemic. We have gone through trenches at work.

'But who am I to complain? Who am I to question her? She was closer to the manager. I was wrong for trusting her and treating her as a friend.' I thought, as I washed the dishes in the back of the kitchen. I sniffed and tried to hold back my tears.

"Are you okay?" Rebecca asked since she heard me sniffing.

I was betrayed by someone I thought was loyal to me. Someone I felt I could trust, someone I thought was my friend and whom I felt I could lean on. I was still figuring out the reason why she betrayed me. My feelings could not accept it.

'But what do I do with it? Should I take revenge against her? Should I cut off our friendship? Should I cut off Jeyja for betraying me? I don't know.' I thought.

I looked up to Rebecca and said, "No."

I wanted to ask Jeyja why she had to tell Antonio about it.

'Can't she keep her mouth shut and pretend she didn't hear what I vented about? Everyone has something against each other at work.' I thought.

Thoughts running through my mind non-stop. I had a lot of questions to ask Jeyja. I couldn't understand why she told Antonio everything I said.

'What did she gain? Perhaps Antonio was more important to her than our friendship.' I thought.

I wanted to take revenge against Jeyja for being a "snake" traitor and my manager for being too much of a hypocrite, but I didn't know how to take revenge. All I could think of was posting my thoughts on social media against Antonio and Jeyha.

In May 2020, Antonio added me on social media, which was bizarre to me, but of course, I accepted his friend request, and it was my biggest mistake. I learned that we shouldn't have our co-workers on our social media because it is supposed to be a safe space for us. But since my manager added me, he could see my whereabouts and what I posted.

Back then, I didn't know how to hide posts from certain people on Facebook. Since he could see my story, he could indulge in my social media posts. I voiced my anger about my manager on social media, saying, "It's funny how you posted much about being a family and leader at work, yet you don't know how to make a stand."

Macy knew who I was talking about. But in the end, even though I vented out on social media, I couldn't do much about it other than that. I felt weak because I didn't know how to fight back. I could only vent about them with other people who knew them. I still worked diligently and carried that hurt within me as I worked.

"This shall come to pass; I just need some time for the wound to heal." I thought to myself.

50

FORGIVING

My hands shook every time I thought about Jeyja for betraying me. It cut deep in my heart every time I thought about her. She was one of the loveliest people I have ever worked with, and we hung out at work. We shared our life stories together and helped each other at work. Yet, in the end, I realized that no one is perfect, and people have a choice to be loyal friends or not.

I let myself hold onto my grudges. I got hurt so many times in life that my heart became as hard as a stone. I thought hardening my heart and not forgiving someone would protect it from getting hurt, but it was the other way around.

I saw a social media post about a snake and the axe story.

The snake accidentally cut himself with an axe, and the snake got mad at the axe for cutting him. The snake took revenge by wrapping the axe with its body; as the snake wrapped the blade of the axe, it cut the snake's body even more. The snake thought that the axe was trying to fight back, but the snake didn't have any idea that by wrapping its body around the axe or taking revenge, the snake was only hurting themselves. In the end, the snake died.

In the story, the snake symbolizes those who got hurt, and the axe symbolizes those who hurt us. A similar situation can happen when we take revenge; we only hurt ourselves. Instead of forgiving people who hurt us, we only add a scar to our hearts.

I was hurt, but I told myself that it was okay as long as I was the one who got hurt than the one hurting somebody else. Everything has an end point. I always tell myself that everything on earth is temporary and everything shall pass. I hate to say this, but we don't know when our last day will be. We all are going to leave this world one day. Any possessions and things we have will not come to the grave with us.

As for me, I got hurt many times in life, but that is how I learn. Perhaps a tiny piece of my broken self has taught me that I only destroy myself more when I take revenge. Another piece of my broken self has taught me that neither I nor my co-workers were perfect, and the rest of my broken self has taught me to forgive and be kind despite how cruel this world is. Forgiving people is one of the hardest things to do. Forgiving is not only for those who hurt you but also to make space for your healing and to make peace with yourself.

51

GOODBYE, BRUNO

I woke up at 04:30 in the morning with a message from Bruno.

"I'm sorry I can't love you how you deserve to be loved. I'm in a place where I need to go home, and I don't know if I'll ever return to Canada."

His message brought a tear to my eye. Even though I felt a sense of loss, deep down, I was happy for him as he would finally be with his family. I hadn't opened his message yet; I had read it from my phone's notification. Memories from when we met in Port Credit while walking by the lake, our conversations at the restaurant, and how we held hands and kissed suddenly flooded my mind.

I sat on my bed while everyone at home was asleep. My surroundings were silent. I could hear my cat's snoring somewhere in my dark room. I checked the flights from Toronto to Zagreb, Croatia. It was expensive for me, especially for someone who earns a minimum wage.

I had a morning shift scheduled at 07:00. I knew I needed more sleep but didn't want to go back to sleep. I read articles online on how to move on from a heartbreak, but I couldn't read them properly because I couldn't focus on them. I left my room, prepared for work, and fed my cat. I went back to reading Bruno's message from my phone's notification.

'What should I say?' I asked myself.

When I was ready for work at 06:30, I took three deep breaths, opened his message and replied,

"It's okay, Bruno. I understand, and I respect you. You'll always have a place in my heart; it's as cheesy as it sounds. I'm happy that I have met you. Take care of yourself."

I was about to cry but had to suppress my feelings because I had to call an Uber and go to work. Bruno had given me many hints that he didn't like me, which was hard for me to accept.

In 2020, he told me he could not love me how I deserved to be loved. His words manifested through his actions, indicating that he didn't like me. We would fight through text messages because of misunderstandings, and in return, I had to apologize because I misinterpreted him.

As a young adult, I was very keen on marriage. I dreamed of getting married and having kids one day. But with the lifestyle that Bruno and I had grown up with, we weren't a great match. Bruno was older than me, and I trusted him more than I trusted myself. I let him lead our situationship, and he led me to the end of our situationship. Although it was hard to accept, from time to time, I decided to take our fate that we weren't meant to be together.

When I got off my Uber ride that day to start my opening shift, I tried forgetting about his message and his departure from Canada by thinking about what I needed to do first in the morning for my work duty. Jena and Chris were already in the store. I sipped from my coffee cup and greeted Jena and Chris,

"Good morning."

I took my hairnet, dropped my bag in the breakroom, and sipped my coffee again. I went to the kitchen and started preparing the food items. I did my usual morning routine in the store as if nothing bothered me, but deep inside, my heart was wretched because of what Bruno said.

While preparing burger patties, I secretly checked my phone in the kitchen and saw that he liked the message I sent to end our conversation. I washed my hands and realized I hadn't punched in for my shift fifteen minutes after starting work.

"I forgot to punch in!" I exclaimed.

"Oh no, oh no, oh no-no-no-no- no!" Chris said, mocking the song that Antonio always used on his Facebook story.

We all laughed!

After punching my time for my work shift, I went back to making burger patties. I stared at the sizzling patties blankly.

'Should I go to Croatia? Maybe one day, I'd meet him again.' I thought, still hopeful. I was overwhelmed with emotions, feeling as though my heart was being torn apart as I came to terms with the fact that he was leaving Canada.

"The other side of the patties are almost burnt, and you need to flip them," Jena said.

"Oh, yeah," I said, then flipped the burger patties.

"Are you okay? Haha. You're like an idiot there staring at the patties." Jena said. We both laughed. "You don't blink your eyes. Haha."

"Haha. Just going through some rough road." I replied.

"Hahaha. I think you're still sleeping. Are you still dreaming?" Jena said.

As much as I wanted to tell Chris and Jena about Bruno, I knew they wouldn't understand despite being my close friends. I hid what I felt by laughing and joking.

Chris heard that we were laughing and asked, "What happened?"

"Sis Rainna is daydreaming. Hahaha!" Jena said.

"Hahaha! I am still in my dreams while the patties are burning," I said, trying to give them a hint of what was going on with me. "He's gone through, just like my feelings for him. Hahaha."

"Ouhhh… Who is it? Your bebe, the military guy? Hahaha!" said Chris.

"Hahaha, none. Just like my feelings for him. Hahaha." I exclaimed in a matter as if cancelling my own emotions. I finished making patties and went to the dine-in area to wipe the tables. Then I said, "Everything has an end."

"Ohh, sis Rainna got some *hugot*. Hahaha." Jena said.

We laughed. While deeply inside me, my heart was falling apart.

When Bruno returned to Croatia a week after he sent me that parting message, he posted pictures and videos on his Instagram story and saw that he was happier.

'*It was great, Bruno, until it lasted.*' I thought.

I was pleased for him, though I wish I had gone there with him. But it wouldn't change the fact that we were not meant to be together and weren't made for each other.

To soothe my pain, I listened to melancholic melodies that resonated with my inner turmoil. The idea of travelling to Croatia crossed my mind, sparking a glimmer of hope that I might meet him again. However, learning the Croatian language (Hrvatski) could be challenging. The thought of leaving behind my life in Canada weighed heavily on my chest.

I fell in love with Bruno and waited several years for him to love me. Then, I had fallen in love, and I realized that everything that fell shattered into pieces.

52

CARPE DIEM

One of my favourite movies is Dead Poet Society (1989). Robin Williams plays the role of John Keating, a new English teacher with a unique teaching style. He lets his students read books outside the classroom and look at the pictures displayed in school.

As his students looked at the displayed pictures, John Keating said, "Carpe Diem."

Carpe diem means "seize the day." or "pluck the day".

The Roman poet Horace used the phrase to express that one should enjoy life while one can. It means enjoying the day and taking the time to enjoy each second of your life.

After filling the cups with soft drinks, I cut the drink trays in half. For half an hour, the store was not busy, and the surroundings were quiet; the people in the kitchen were not talking to each other. However, everyone at the store was doing something.

"Rainna, you can go on your ten-minute break while it's not busy," Adrianna said.

"Okay, I'm gonna get my food," I replied and chose my food.

She went to the office to get her swiping card. "Okay, what would you like to get?" Adrianna asked.

"Just mashed potatoes and a piece of chicken and bottled water," I said.

"You sure you can finish eating it in 10 minutes?" Adrianna in her reassuring voice.

"Yeah, I'm hungry right now," I said as I removed the plastic gloves from my hands.

While Adrianna was preparing my food, I washed my hands thoroughly. As I was washing my hands, some memories of the pre-pandemic lingered in my mind. I remember not having to wear a mask and gloves while working. Our store was full of people eating and laughing.

'Time flies so fast. I couldn't take the years back, and I couldn't be sure about the future.' I thought. After washing my hands, I turned the tap water off with paper towels.

When I received my food, I went to the break room and noticed that the kitchen floor was slippery because water splashed from the sink. Then, cardboard boxes were placed on the floor to soak up the water. I didn't have time to check my phone; I had to eat faster within 10 minutes. I finished eating 12 minutes later, and when I returned to the front, Chase was there looking through the window glass, and it wasn't busy.

"It's so quiet. Who wants to go home?" Adrianna said jokingly.

Our supervisors tend to send us home early when work isn't busy. Since it wasn't that busy, I went to our break room, grabbed my phone, and went to the washroom. I checked my phone to see if someone had sent me a message. I checked my Facebook, and there was a "memory to look back" from two years ago when we went hiking with my family.

I thought, *'We can't take back the years that have passed and cannot be sure about our future. All we have right now is our present; what matters is how we spend our day.'*

When I came out of the washroom, one of my co-workers stood outside, waiting for me to come out.

'I hope he didn't wait too long,' I worried.

I placed my phone back in my bag and went to the storefront. I washed my hands again and noticed the paper towel dispenser was empty. I didn't have a key to change the dispenser, so I had no choice but to air-dry my hands. I wore plastic gloves and walked to the cash register, where I took the customer who only ordered large fries. We had two customers, and Chase was taking the other customer.

'Be present, no matter how bad your job is or how much you want to quit.' I thought. Thoughts of quitting were lingering in my mind. But savouring every moment helped me retain my job and be thankful for a chance to work during the pandemic.

Working at a fast-food restaurant for seven years in total was brutal, although I chose to work in that field. I have seen the worst, been treated unfairly, had terrible experiences, and encountered the most unexpected instances an employee could witness. But I had to remind myself to be present at the moment, no matter how bad my job was or how much I wanted to quit. I had to be patient because everything would come to pass.

If I didn't feel like working, I would work mindlessly or on autopilot. Working on autopilot means doing enough work and being okay, and it won't hurt me to change my pace.

I would come to work, sign in on the clock, and wish for the hours to go faster. I would see the customers as my enemies and take orders quickly, asking them, "Anything else?" so they would not add more items to their orders. I wanted to be disconnected at the moment when working. I wanted to be deaf and not hear anything in the realm of reality.

I didn't want to be there. I didn't want to work, but I still had bills to pay. I couldn't just quit with no other plans afterwards because no one would hire me if I did. All businesses and malls were closed. The world was in a total shutdown era during the pandemic.

My job at a fast-food restaurant was all I had. I felt like I was in a cage, trapped where I couldn't move and left with no option but to live a little. I felt suffocated, and I felt limited.

When everything shuts down, I learned to live in chaos. I learned how to thrive, live in the moment and be grateful. The point of *carpe diem* is to enjoy life while we can.

I talked to Jan when there were no customers in the store, and I told him the story of my former co-worker at my previous job.

"He left on his break time and never returned for the rest of his shift on his last day. Hahaha!"

"That's gonna be you when you quit Fast Food. Hahaha!" Jan said.

"I'm going to throw my hat on the floor, step on it, and say, 'I quit!' Haha!" I said, joking to Jan.

"Yeah! Goodbye, m*ther f*ckaas!" he replied.

Jan and I knew we wouldn't rudely leave Fast Food. We just imagined how we would want to quit and how we would like to act when we finally leave our Fast Food job. We joked a lot about quitting and how we hated the job but still stayed in the job we hated. But I remember from the Dead Poet Society movie, Robin Williams also said in the film, "sucking the marrow out of life doesn't mean choking on the bone." It means we don't have to put ourselves in a bad situation to seize the day. *Carpe diem* does not mean blasting out in the wrong way. It simply means to enjoy the day and not put ourselves at risk. I realized that if I were ever going to quit my job, I would want to leave pleasantly and respectfully, even though I've had bad experiences. There were moments when I enjoyed this job, and I found my people at Fast Food.

53

OUR TRUE WORK IS LOOKING AFTER ONE ANOTHER

At the beginning of 2022, I was juggling two full-time jobs. I got a job as a COVID-19 Tester at nursing home while I was still working at fast food. My usual work schedule was six days at Fast Food and five days in the healthcare field. My only day off from both jobs was during Saturdays.

Rebecca brought me my favourite breakfast from the next-door market. The meal has rice, eggs, and *longanisa*, a Filipino sausage. She knew that I always buy that for breakfast. It was in the middle of the week, and she came by to give that food to me. I was tired and hungry when she came, and it was the perfect moment when she arrived and brought me food and a handwritten note that said:

"FOR YOU, *BAKLA*."

She wrote some encouraging words for me to keep going. "*Bakla*" means "gay" in Tagalog or Filipino language. We call each other "gay" as an endearment.

I was pleasantly surprised when she showed up with breakfast and a handwritten letter for me. I truly value the effort she put into writing a letter. In a world where I'm constantly using technology to communicate, receiving a letter from a dear friend like Rebecca feels wonderfully nostalgic and heartwarming.

She sent me a text message later that night, saying,

"I noticed you are not the same energetic Rainna I know." She included a sad emoji in her text message.

I will never forget what Rebecca did because someone like her made me feel seen and valued when no one noticed. Although Rebecca and I were friends outside of work, Rebecca taught me to look after co-workers and treat anyone as a human being, whether they were the manager, supervisor, team leader, or crew member.. My co-workers get tired like me; they have family and kids, fall in love, and have feelings like any individual. My co-workers are not robots; they are there at my workplace to work, provide for their families and themselves, and pay bills just like you me. I realized that beside the actual job at work, our true work is to look after one another. Working as a team means helping with workloads and looking after one another's state of mind. We don't know what our co-workers were going through. Sometimes, they could smile and laugh, but they may break deep inside. We don't know what they are going through in their heads. Some of them may want to give up in life. We won't know until we check up on them. Rebecca was more than a co-worker, she was a sister, and a good friend.

⚘⚘⚘

I was going through difficulties in life. I lacked sleep, my body was in pain, and I couldn't get up every morning. I wanted to call in sick, and I also fought with Marsha. She thought I was working at her station in the kitchen and did not clean it. She yelled at me for not cleaning her station and gave me a dirty look. She started working at five o'clock in the afternoon every weekday and had another job.

When Marsha arrived at work, she saw me making a few burgers. She initially thought I had worked at the burger station since the store opened and didn't clean her station afterwards. But I worked at the storefront until my Indian co-worker went for her break. I only had to make two burgers because no one was making them.

"I wasn't working here; I worked at the front," I said.

She screamed at me, "Even though! Whoever worked here should clean the station."

I was fed up and didn't have the energy to fight with her. I went to the front and started taking orders. I heard Marsha having tantrums and slamming the sauce and boxes at her station. I listened to her cussing and saying that I was dirty.

I wanted to cry because one of my pet peeves was being blamed for what I didn't do. I was not at her station until I had to make a few burgers, which took me only 5 minutes. I used her station for only 5 minutes. Another worker who had worked there since morning caused the mess and left empty sauce containers.

'Why would she throw her anger at me? I didn't even stay there longer than 5 minutes and wouldn't make such a mess within 5 minutes!' I thought. *'Her anger was not for me; her tantrums shouldn't carry me away. I didn't make any mess there. I will cry later.'*

I then worked on autopilot for two hours until my shift was done. I wasn't feeling well; my heart felt heavy, and I was holding back my tears. The store got busy, yet I was still checking the clock because I was looking forward to going home. I didn't want to be sensitive because I was hurt and needed to stay strong for the rest of my shift.

Ten minutes before my shift ended, I cleaned the counter and stocked the front store. I punched out and didn't talk to anyone. I saw Marsha gave me a dirty look. I rolled my eyes at her in return.

I cautiously made my way through the bustling kitchen. The tiled floor was wet, and every step had to be deliberate to prevent slips or falls. Meanwhile, my co-worker Andrew diligently pressed carton boxes onto the damp surface, allowing them to soak up the spill. As he worked, he casually conversed with other workers, their voices mixing with the soft swishing of the boxes against the floor.

When I arrived home that night, I felt a heavy weight on my chest. The day had been exhausting, and I wanted to relieve the stress. I turned on the shower, feeling the warm water wash over me, easing the tension in my muscles. After I dried off, I wore my favourite comfortable sleepwear, a soft old t-shirt and worn-in pyjama pants.

As I got ready for bed, my mind was filled with emotions. I found myself searching for painkillers or something to numb the ache I felt inside. It made me question if I needed to return to therapy. Eventually, I lay down and closed my eyes, hoping that sleep would relieve the overwhelming emotions that consumed me. Despite wanting to cry, I chose to sleep, seeking a temporary escape from the unfathomable feelings that plagued me.

I had to get up early the next day to start a Monday opening shift, but I usually get to work late. I felt happier on the weekdays since I wouldn't have to see Marsha. I only see Marsha on Sundays since I work until four o'clock in the afternoon, but sometimes, I stay for a few hours at work when needed.

I was stressed about my finances, even though I knew I was secure with two full-time jobs. I felt weak, insecure, and depressed. The only person I could share my problems with was Rebecca. She always had listening ears, and I could vent to Rebecca about almost anything and everything happening in my life.

Antonio noticed that I had been coming in late for days. He talked to me for the last time in the office and asked me what was going on with me. I was always late for work, but I was completely different.

I told him I was working two full-time jobs because I needed money and was burnt out. I also told him I fought with Marsha, which added to my sadness and because of the weight I felt and burned out, I cried in front of Antonio.

'What the heck? Why am I crying in front of Antonio? Why didn't I cry when I was alone in my room?' I thought.

I never got a chance to cry out in silence. But the moment when Antonio talked to me, I just let myself be vulnerable. I allowed myself to feel and show my weakness in front of Antonio. I couldn't hold my tears, and I could not wait. I could have cried when I walked down the bus stop, but I could not. When I stopped bawling my eyes, Antonio said,

"You need to find out why you need to work two full-time jobs and stick to that."

He kept talking for half an hour, telling me my work performance was deteriorating. While he spoke, I realized I needed to be excellent in both jobs; I couldn't compromise one job over the other because my body wouldn't be able to keep up.

I told Rebecca about my conversation with Antonio and how embarrassed I was to cry in front of him:

"I bawled my eyes 'cause I was burnt out and couldn't help it," I told Rebecca.

"That's okay, Bakla. Take it easy. You need to rest, and it's not worth killing yourself at the job that pays you minimum." Rebecca said in her encouraging tone.

The next day, I called in sick at my other job in the medical field for the first time. I was honest with them by telling them,

"I felt weak and sick, but I don't have COVID-19. I haven't slept properly for a few days but will return tomorrow."

They were friendly and understood me. They had found someone else to cover my shift. I knew I needed to be stronger. I had to work two full-time jobs, not because I wanted to but needed to. Perhaps I wouldn't have survived my work without Rebecca. I would appreciate and tell Rebecca how grateful I am to meet her, even if there was no occasion. I occasionally told her how thankful I am to her; she told me once, "Fast food might be a sh*ttiest place, but I've met great people there, including you."

54

GOODBYE, FAST-FOOD

'I need to hand in my resignation this week.' I thought.

I had been thinking of giving my resignation a month early instead of two weeks' notice because Antonio asked Kathy and Chase to stay for a while after their two weeks' notice. I thought they needed some people to hire, and I didn't want to burden them when I left.

'My resignation letter has to be funny.' I thought.

When I got home, my mom asked me to prepare my COVID-19 vaccination, passport, and ID since we were going to the Philippines for a month's vacation. I printed out my COVID-19 vaccination and researched the guidelines for travelling.

Macy and her family travelled during the high-risk pandemic and had to stay in a hotel for two weeks. Since they had loosened up a bit with precaution when we travelled to the Philippines, we only needed to provide our vaccination record and the questionnaire online we had to answer before travelling outside Canada. We didn't have to quarantine for two weeks like Macy and her family did.

I prepared the things I needed for my vacation, and then I prepared my resignation letter.

As I typed in my address and my name on the resignation letter, I realized that perhaps God had put me in a situation where I faced difficulties, not to punish me but to make me realize and see the wounds as art and find beauty in unpleasing moments. God trusted me with the job and the place where He put me to work because I needed to learn something that I wouldn't learn elsewhere. Those good and bad experiences have shaped who I am today.

'When I face difficulties at my future job, I'll remember how I overcame the obstacles I have endured at this job,' I thought.

The next day, I had a day off and went out with my family. Antonio messaged me on Facebook and asked, "Would you like to be a supervisor?".

I didn't reply to him immediately because I wanted to enjoy my time with my family then. I was shivering in the cold and could not type on my phone properly because I wore winter gloves, and I didn't want to take off.

'I need to think this through.' I thought. My heart was a drumbeat, pounding out rhythms of exhilaration as I drank a hot chocolate.

I had considered taking the supervisory position, but I knew I would quit and my time at a fast-food restaurant would end. When we went home with my family a few hours later, I replied to Antonio and declined the offer.

'I don't need this position. I better give that position to people who need it,' I thought.

I knew some of my co-workers would need that supervisory position experience to gain permanent residence in Canada. Besides, I had another full-time job, which was in my field.

I thought, *'I've had enough with fast food. It's been seven years.'.*

I was eager to write my thoughts in my journal that night since I was getting emotional. I thought, '*If I could return, I would still choose to work at a fast-food restaurant, even if I knew how hard and worse it would be.*'

I could not believe I was quitting fast food sooner rather than later. I had another full-time job, and my favourite people, such as Rolland, Charles, Kathy, Naveena, Chase, Norman, Nessa, and Nelia, quit fast food before me; sometimes, it wasn't the same working at fast food without them. Other people I worked with during the pandemic impacted me for the better.

My life as a fast-food worker has taught me a lot. I don't know how many things it taught me, but I wouldn't change my job for anything about my experience working at a fast-food restaurant. Working at a fast-food restaurant for seven years has helped me become who I am today. If I could go back in time, I would do it again.

This time, I am closing this chapter. Part of closing this chapter is forgiving Jeyja. Her betrayal remained a mystery and hurtful experience for me, and I struggled to understand why she had to do that. It left me puzzled in many ways and caused me distress. Despite that, I realized that holding onto the pain was only causing me stress. So, after a long process and dealing with my feelings and confusion, I decided to work on forgiving her to find peace within myself.

Also, as part of closing this chapter, I wouldn't forget what *Mariano* had caused me and the people who made false accusations about me about having an affair with *Mariano*. Still, I will always be grateful that they fired him. I was still weak in faith and didn't desire to read the Word of God like I used to, but I'm giving credit to God since He made a way for me to take me out of that storm. The only hope I had was Jesus Christ. Although my faith was in a messy place, I prayed earnestly to God to deliver me from the ugly situation I was in. I remember Jesus' parable about the Mustard seed. We could move mountains with faith as small as the mustard seed. I had faith as small as a mustard seed, and God watered it for me. I had faith in God. I still believed in God. He has answered my prayer by giving me symptoms of COVID-19. It was not something I wanted to have, but it was a way to ease the heat between *Mariano* and me. If I didn't have COVID-19 symptoms, I wouldn't have taken a break, and it would make the heat more intense between us.

Rainna Ancheta

8th May 2022

RE: Resignation Letter

Dear Management,

I quit.

My last day will be on the 5th of June.

Thank you.

Sincerely,

Rainna Ancheta   08/05/2022

55

PANDEMIC REFLECTION

During the pandemic, customers heavily relied upon fast-food workers. Working as an essential worker during the pandemic proved to be a challenging experience, but it taught me to be grateful for what I had instead of complaining. Despite working six days a week, I was thankful for a job that sustained my basic needs and helped me survive. I learned to be grateful for the little things I have and live to the fullest.

Before worrying about certain things, we must be grateful for what we currently have. Even if we're not working our dream job or have not been contacted for an interview, it's essential to appreciate the job that we currently have as it sustains our lives and helps us survive. Whatever our job may be, we should be thankful for it.

Sometimes, while doing mundane tasks like cleaning the store or taking customers' complaints, we may reevaluate our lives and realize we're not where we want to be. However, it's important to remember that we're in the right place and don't need to compare ourselves to others. We'll all have our winning moments eventually.

As a fast-food worker during the pandemic, I had to remind customers to wear masks upon entering our store for an eight-hour shift, which could be tiring. However, I reminded myself that there were still things to be grateful for despite the challenges. No matter what we're worried about, we should never forget that there's something to be thankful for. I was grateful when I worked at the fast food restaurant and enjoyed working there. I loved my co-workers; they were why our work was not a job but a work to socialize and make memories with. Although not everyone liked me at work and was nice to me, my co-workers helped me work and forget about the world briefly.

But sometimes, during my break time at work, I couldn't stop thinking about how my life would be if I didn't work. What would life be like if I had parents to provide for my needs? Would I be living my best life? Would staying at home and having everyone work for me be fulfilling? Those questions were running inside my head while sitting in the breakroom.

I realized that there is no easy life, and despite working at a fast food restaurant during the pandemic, I found a fulfilling life. Despite the experience, and probably the worst, if I could get a chance, I would go back to experience living an undesirable life; I found beauty amid sadness and difficulties. I took every life lesson I learned while working at a fast-food restaurant during the pandemic.

When I got home, I had many realizations in life. As I approached my last weeks at a fast-food restaurant and wrote my resignation letter, the memories from December 2019 to May 2022 lingered in my mind, and I could not help but let my tears out of my eyes. The tears streamed down my face, not of sadness but of joy. I had finally said that I had survived a chaotic life experience.

Perhaps a fast-food restaurant is a stepping stone for some, but for me, it was a place to grow, a place to meet great people, and a place where I would go back in time and show my future kids and grandkids where I used to work during the pandemic and where the voices lie. As a fast food worker, I had to be of service. I had to serve my customers well and do the right job. I worked hard even though nobody noticed me. I gave my best shots when working because work is not about getting the most money or getting into a higher position but about being of service.

During the most challenging situation, I learned to live as if you are not afraid of tomorrow. Part of living a life to the fullest is to be grateful. I learned to be thankful for what I have. As a 22-year-old working at a fast-food restaurant during the pandemic, I felt insecure and left behind in life. However, I realized how lucky I was to have a job. Not having everything figured out made life more adventurous. I learned to be thankful for the small things, like my job, family, and co-workers.

※※※

As of July 2022, there have been seven waves of the pandemic in Canada. We still wore masks but didn't have to pay attention to the six-foot distances. I honestly ignored how many waves we had.

When I quit a fast-food restaurant, I threw a party at my house. I didn't remove my uniform because I knew it would be my last day wearing it.

Two days after the quitting party, Rebecca and I celebrated our birthdays at CN Tower in Toronto. Our birthdays are in June, and we're no doubt best friends. She paid for everything, and we enjoyed the view. We enjoyed taking pictures from the great view from the CN Tower.

My grandma, mom, and I went to the Philippines for vacation three days later. It was my first time coming back home after nine years. Some of my friends had work jobs, and I could not believe we were once in our early teens, trying to figure out our future. All of a sudden, 9 years later, we had our jobs. None of my friends were getting married anytime soon, but some were in a healthy relationship, and some were still single. I have missed a part of their lives. I have missed a lot of birthdays and Christmas with them. But they all have a place in my heart.

My high school friends in the Philippines and I talked about COVID-19 and how they lost their jobs and stayed at home. Some of them managed to work from home. We discussed how acne covered their faces because they wore masks in hot weather. We talked about relationships, work, and family.

One of my goals in the Philippines is to have alone time alone. I asked my mom if we had anywhere to go so I could go on indoor rock climbing by myself. But we had to leave every day to visit places. But there was a day when we didn't have to go anywhere but sleep because we were going to the province at night. I took the chance to get alone by myself and went indoor rock climbing before the night we were leaving. I left around noon. I stayed at indoor rock climbing for two hours, then I went to the coffee shops nearby. I then reflected on my life.

I was proud of myself for conquering difficulties. When I went to Canada, I only thought I would be working once I was 16. I never thought I would be working at a fast-food restaurant. I never thought a lot could happen in nine years. Although I was not getting a high-pay rate as I thought I would be getting, I am grateful for all of my experiences in life. I have conquered much in life.

Being grateful is about appreciating what you have and being content. It doesn't mean you can't move forward and achieve more. Living a life to the fullest means being alive in each moment you have. You may have your definition of life, but do whatever makes you feel alive. Live as if it is your last day. While you can still stand firm on both feet, do the things that you are scared of because one day, you'll be on your deathbed, and all you'll have is your memories.

Conclusion

My mother always said, "The earth is round. Sometimes you are at the top, and sometimes you are at the bottom.". You won't always be on the bottom and not on top. When you reach the rock bottom of your life, know you will get on top and won't stay at the bottom. Life has ups and downs; life is like a wheel because the world is always turning.

Every one of us has a different lens. Even my co-workers, though I worked with them, might have different lenses than I did. They might have learned something different than me.

Everyone went through a hard time during that year in 2020. The years gone by since 2020 were fast. Life is not easy, but it is getting better. As you get older, you get wiser, just like a fine wine, and when you are in the season of learning, embrace it.

I have carried these life lessons with me until now. I became more aware of myself and my surroundings. I didn't get therapy after my 3-month therapy in 2020 because, throughout the years, I carried everything that my therapist, Julia, had taught me. I learned to enjoy the moment I have. Every time I drink coffee in the morning, I pause and appreciate life. I appreciate everything that I have, even the most minor things.

The year 2020 might be the worst year to most of us, but as for me, I have learned a lot during those hard times.

⇓⇓⇓

Through the lens of my co-workers during the pandemic.

I shared a question sticker on my Instagram account, posting it only to a closed friends list who worked with me during the pandemic. Only three people responded to it. Most of them didn't want to revisit a memory in 2020 since it had been a traumatizing year for them. I asked some of my co-workers in direct message and asked them about what good memories they won't forget while working at fast food during the pandemic. Beside the traumatic experience during the pandemic as a fast food worker, there were good memories that we had shared with one another.

What is something unforgettable for you working at a fast-food restaurant during the pandemic?

There were lots of customer fights I would not forget. –Jeyja

"When we work the same shift, we all know what to do." – Jennica

"When we work together" -Macy

"Of course when I worked with you 'cause you're gay! HAHAHA" - Jena

"When Lolita quit from fastfood! When I hosted a colouring contest between production and service team, and when Nelia bought cakes for team members" - Nessa

"When we bought coffees and shared with work best friends every paycheck, and when we played AmongUs after work." Chris

"Bonding with the crew after work!" -Ralph

Acknowledgement

Thank you, Milton & Hugo, for the book cover design and for bringing this book to life. Thank you for all the help, communicating with me and answering all my queries.

Thank you, Emi, for everything you did, for your "hugot" emails, for answering my questions, for helping me understand what I needed to know, and for all the hard work you put into making my debut memoir memorable.

Thank you to my family—mom, dad, and older brothers—and trusted friends Bryan, Angel, and Mariel for helping me pick a title I was undecided about. Thank you for all your support with my writing and helping me on this journey.

Thank you, Egzon, for assisting me with the final edits and supporting me. I appreciate being able to trust you with the manuscript and for informing me of what I needed to change.

Thank you, Chris, Jeyja, Nessa, Norman, and Naveena, for helping me dig up the memories we didn't want to remember at work. I greatly appreciate you all taking the time to remember our shared memories.

Thank you to everyone I worked with at a fast-food restaurant during the pandemic. I may not remember all your names and faces, but I will never forget how much we thrived working together during the most challenging times.

Thank you to my editor for helping me with the book's manuscript and for the love and effort you put into my debut memoir. Thank you for taking care of it when I couldn't. You will always have a big part in this book.

Praise For Behind The Plexiglass

"I laughed so much at you telling the story of how awful that customer who ordered the 10 burgers and then said, Where are the drinks?! You relayed that story very well. It gives us a good insight into the Pandemic, how hard you all worked, and how the customers took their stress out on you who were also trying to deal with it. It was fun to read, but I also felt for you in your job. It was a stressful time. You did an amazing job. Well done!" - Orla K, Writer and Life Coach

Rainna's story during the Pandemic sends a sense of comfort, letting us know that all of us struggled in our own different ways— whether we stayed at home during the Pandemic or we went out to work to serve other people. She gave us a different facet of view on her version of daily life as a fast food worker; that they're also people like us who has needs, problems to take care of and were seeking times to chill in a difficult time as well. Her story is very relatable and yet unique in a precious way! - Angelica T, Makeup Artist and Editor

"I did not expect to read a story almost the same as mine. As I read this, it brought back memories and trauma of 2020. I have never felt so emotional while reading, but this made me cry, and the anger I felt that year came back." - Jebilyn

"It is interesting reading another person's experience, especially since mine is different." -Aleksandra

"I love how you go into details with the situation and explain." - Egzon

"My honest review of this book is that you chose the topic and were to the point, as well as detailed where the readers can relate themselves who worked as front liners during the pandemic days. It can be read in one sitting. I found it interesting how you portrayed your real experiences in this." - Nisha

Notes

Prologue

https://www.canada.ca/en/employment-social-development/programs/ei.html

https://www.thestar.com/politics/a-timeline-of-covid-19-in-canada/article_825f5047-a427-5336-8c9c-0463dcfb9469.html

https://www.who.int/health-topics/coronavirus#tab=tab_1

https://www.thecanadianencyclopedia.ca/en/article/pandemic

Chapter 1

https://www.nytimes.com/2021/10/21/books/review/review-the-road-by-cormac-mccarthy.html

https://www.thecanadianencyclopedia.ca/en/article/covid-19-pandemic

Chapter 2

https://www.cnn.com/us/live-news/kobe-bryant-dies-in-helicopter-crash/index.html

https://www.elephantjournal.com/2021/01/a-life-lesson-that-kobe-bryant-left-us/

Chapter 4

https://www.sciencenews.org/article/australia-wildfires-climate-change-carbon-dioxide-ocean-algae

Chapter 16

https://www.psychologytoday.com/us/blog/two-takes-depression/201403/7-big-stupid-destructive-lies-depression-tells-you

Chapter 21

https://www.medicalnewstoday.com/articles/what-is-pcr-test#uses

Chapter 31

https://pmc.ncbi.nlm.nih.gov/articles/PMC8662215/#:~:text=During%20the%20COVID%E2%80%9019%20pandemic%2C%2045.35%25%20of%20the%20participants,on%20the%20chin%20(78.26%25)

https://www.medicalnewstoday.com/articles/stress-hormones

https://www.mdpi.com/2079-9284/10/6/146

Chapter 52

https://www.britannica.com/topic/carpe-diem

About The Author

Rainna Ancheta is a Filipino-Canadian writer and has written over 200 articles online since 2021. She published about faith, life lessons, life stories and self-improvement. She has worked at a fast-food restaurant for seven years at two different companies since immigrating to Canada. In March 2021, she was interviewed by OMNI News to share her firsthand experience as a fast-food employee during the pandemic. Rainna has contributed to platform such as Thought Catalog, Collective World, and Elephant Journal. Additionally, Rainna is a certified creative writer, having successfully completed both a 15-week writing workshop at the Living Arts Centre Mississauga in 2018 and a 10-week writing workshop at the University of Toronto in 2024.

Social Media

Instagram:
@behindtheplexiglass
@rainnawrites

X (Former Twitter):
@rainnawrites

FaceBook Page:
rainnawrites

Website:
Medium.com
https://rainnaaanne.medium.com/

Contact me:
rainnainkpress@gmail.com

www.ingramcontent.com/pod-product-compliance
Lightning Source LLC
Chambersburg PA
CBHW032100090426
42743CB00007B/192